This book is dedicated to
my parents, Anne and
George Bellef, who taught
me to never walk past a
second-hand store without
taking a quick look inside.

Individual

Individual

Inspiration for creating a home
that is uniquely your own

Jessica Bellef

murdoch books
Sydney | London

Contents

Sandra Eterovic sadly passed away before the printing of this book. I am grateful to her family and her partner for allowing the publication of her story.

J.B.

Introduction

We all deserve to live unapologetically in homes that are a true reflection of who we are, within spaces that make us feel connected, emotionally rich and secure. As we strive for more meaning and authenticity in our lives, it's real homes that inspire and energise us. This book is a celebration of creative people and individual approaches to interior design. It highlights the unique stories that make us who we are.

What follows on these pages is a snapshot of the variety of ways in which we live. When photographer Sue Stubbs and I set out to document the homes, we knew that it was vital to capture the relationship between the homeowner and their space; the story of each home can't be separated from the story of each individual, as the space is coloured by their motivations, fears and desires.

Each of the case studies proudly shouts out with distinct style and feeling, from a crafty hand-built straw-bale home nestled in rolling hills to a 1970s-era palace in the 'burbs. These homes weren't created by hired interior designers or completely furnished in one transaction at a big-box retailer. The homes—and the collections within them—are autobiographical in nature, layered up over time and subject to the ebb and flow of life.

This book throws out restrictive interior-styling rules and instead offers advice that is practical, realistic and ever so aware of the fact that the most interesting homes are the ones that bend to the whims of the owner and evolve as life rolls on. Instead of listing hard and fast rules, I offer tips and suggestions; I am not here to push certain styles or taste levels, or to say that there is a 'correct' way to decorate.

The instructional element of this book isn't about replicating the homes you see on the pages. You won't find paint colours listed, a stockists' directory at the back of the book or a breakdown of trends and must-have items. What you will find is an exploration of the mindset of individuals who can't help but stamp their own story on their dwellings, and an explanation of why certain homes feel the way they do. This book will help you embrace your individuality and show you how to infuse your spaces with it; the easy and affordable ideas will remain relevant beyond the cycle of meaningless trends.

The people featured in this book follow their hearts and live in spaces that tell their story. Their homes are layered and soulful, textured by daily activities, the serendipity of second-hand finds and the energy of pieces passed down through their families. These people feel good about their homes, because they do whatever the heck they want to them, regardless of financial and spatial limitations or the style du jour touted by tastemakers. I hope their stories inspire you to find your own voice and give you the confidence to bring more of yourself into your home, however that may look or feel.

A city terrace infused with colour and faraway cultures

David

Landscapes by David Whitworth sit on a mantle, while a light fitting by Tord Boontje and an indigo blue painting by David titled *Night Swimming* add drama to the living room (opposite). The previous page features an artwork by Becky Gibson.

David

/

The places we inhabit—momentarily or for the long term—leave us with sensory fragments. A certain slant of light at a specific time of day, the smell of syrupy summer florals growing nearby or an intense colour that lingers even when you close your eyes. These fragments surround David, a painter and landscape architect, in both his career and his home life.

He often works from memory when he paints landscapes, depicting his distilled impression of the location and capturing the essence of colour and light. In his work as a landscape architect, he studies the dialogue between humans and the physical environment; keen to be involved in the process of new memory making for people, his aim is always to create a space that fosters strong connections between nature and culture. As the long-term resident of a share house located a handful of bus stops from Sydney's CBD, David has cultivated a lush garden oasis in the rear courtyard and created an inviting home imprinted with his own experiences and the collective memory of past tenants.

Share houses are usually a mishmash of scrappy furniture and decor, a depressing muddle of miscellaneous origin, but in this share house, meaningful and treasured collections are arranged with an artist's eye. David has lived in the terrace for close to a decade, alongside a rotation of some of his closest friends and art-school buddies. Many a dinner party has been held in this home, countless backyard beers have been sipped and a series of slouchy Sunday mornings have been shared.

The terrace, charmingly dishevelled in parts, contains an impressive gallery of artwork created by previous housemates. The collection documents the home's different eras and combination of personalities, and David—as the unofficial custodian of the home—has meticulously arranged the growing collection in the shared spaces. The careful curation flows into David's bedroom, where art tiles the slate grey walls, bright textiles dress the bed and colourful jewellery and shoes act as eye-catching sculptures.

The unofficial curator of the share house, David loves the irreverence of bright colour and pattern.

A dynamic painting by David decorates this work space. His bedroom (opposite) features artworks by friends and family, as well as unusual bags and sculptural necklaces.

16

David feels that life shouldn't be beige. He painted the dining room turquoise and spray-painted found chairs (opposite), which has brought a fun energy into the space. His earlier artworks (above and opposite) explore the relationship between colour and shape.

David's paintings feature many of the green and blue shades found in the natural environment; however, when it comes to his outfits, there are no limits to the palettes he will blend. He says that his expressive way of dressing is sometimes 'borderline ridiculous', but a shock of unexpected colour and pattern is his way of counterbalancing the seriousness of everyday life. He will finish off an outfit with a vintage kimono bought in Japan, sandals in the colourway of a tropical bird or a scarf he found in a Turkish marketplace.

When it comes to decorating, both sartorially and for the home, David is greatly inspired by the colours, textures and crafts of international cultures. After graduating from art school, he travelled extensively and soaked up the customs of other societies, collecting inspiration, memories and masses of textiles. The share house is filled with David's kanthas, kilims, wedding blankets and embroidered cushions, and the handmade nature of these colourful pieces adds warmth and a layer of story to each space.

David has built up the share house's lush courtyard over time, ramping up his focus on the space when he returned to university to study landscape architecture. His childhood was steeped in plant life; he grew up in homes that backed onto bush, and weekends were spent on nature hikes. The courtyard was originally a completely paved space: depressing, filled with mosquitoes and avoided by the housemates. David instinctively started to re-create the feelings associated with his outdoorsy childhood, building up garden beds, bringing in leafy pot plants and arranging a few different seating areas to break up the space. The large table at the back of the courtyard is perfect for rowdy gatherings, while the smaller table nestled into the narrow laneway is where contemplative alone time happens. The result, a beautiful green antidote to the grey of the surrounding city, is a space that all the housemates utilise.

With his default line of inquiry into the interaction between humans and the physical environment, David has created a beautiful and functional space that enhances life in the terrace. It's a space that the housemates definitely miss when they move out, the flashes of lush green imprinted in their memories.

David and a housemate share breakfast in the narrow laneway that leads to the back courtyard. David's clever redesign of the outdoor areas makes the most of the compact inner-city space.

Housemates appreciate having a garden oasis in the middle of the city. Below, David holds his favourite plant, one that he bought early on during the process of establishing the garden.

Your personal palette and why you should embrace it

Do you know what your favourite colour is? Ask a kid that same question, and the answer is instant and unwavering. As adults, we may have forgotten that an allegiance to a certain shade was symbolic of so much when were young. Declaring a favourite colour was our way of defining ourselves and telling the world what we were about. We requested everything—outfits, bedroom walls, pencil cases, birthday-party decorations—in our chosen chroma. Our hero hues made us happy, even though we were likely to move on to another colour within a month's time.

Fast-forward to our adult years, and we no longer spend time discussing our favourite colours. Sadly, our personal spaces often lack direct reference to the colours that make us joyful. The thing is, we make decisions every day that unconsciously highlight and reinforce the palettes to which we are naturally drawn. From the clothes in our wardrobe to the food we put on our plate (and heck, even the plate itself), our choices about colour continue to tell the story of who we are. If our homes work best for us when they reflect what makes us happy, secure and comforted, then shouldn't we try to inject our own colour palette into the space?

Most interior stylists and designers will tell you that working with colour is the most immediate way to change the mood of a room. Countless articles, workshops and textbooks have delved deep into the technicalities and nuances of colour, breaking the complexities down into rules and prescriptive palettes,

and often not leaving room for creative interpretation. It can be a daunting and stifled way to learn about something that is so personal. It's no wonder that lots of adults are afraid to play with colour in their homes—they're too scared to jump in and express themselves with paint and decor, fearing that they will get it 'wrong'. When it comes to colour, however, it isn't so black and white.

We all have primal, physiological responses to certain colours that we can't control. High-energy reds get the heart racing, while soft blues slow us down. We also have very individual thresholds when it comes to how much colour we can take before nausea sets in. Some people love the feeling of being enveloped in a colour-saturated room, while others would prefer to spend their time in a colour-neutral space.

Our perception of a colour is tinted by our own life story and learned associations. All our memories, positive or negative, will have a connection to colour in some way: the school uniform that was begrudgingly worn, the façade of a crumbling building admired on an exotic holiday, the walls of the dentist's waiting room. It is these fragmented moments that form our preferred colour palettes.

We should unapologetically colour our home environments in palettes that are unique to us, in ways that mean something to us. We need to spend a little time thinking about the colours that give us joy, just as we would have done as bright-eyed young things in the school playground.

> Declaring our favourite colour was a way of defining ourselves when we were young.

Colour considerations

These are not rules, but things to think about:

🌢 Get in tune with the colours to which you react positively. Recall places and moments that made you feel good, and create a mood board (digital or physical) that represents these memories. Take note of recurring colours and themes.

🌢 Adding colour to a room doesn't have to mean you must paint the walls in vibrant hues. Colour can be added to a neutral-walled room through artworks, textiles and decor, and you can add as much or as little as you want.

🌢 Know that you can have too much of a good thing. Overusing one colour in a space will either overwhelm you with its intensity or be so monotonous that you will find the space boring and flat. Play around with a mix of colours in a space until you find a balance that pleases you.

🌢 Understand that paint is temporary and decor is easily swapped out. There is no harm in trying new things, as 'mistakes' can be erased swiftly.

🌢 Observe the scene outside your windows and the way the light works its way through the house. I love having a green quilt cover in my bedroom, as it connects the room to the treetops directly beyond the window, drawing the outside in and grounding me in nature.

🌢 Our preference for certain types of colour will evolve as we grow and advance through our life stages. Embrace these changes, and never stop experimenting with colour in your home.

Objects and colour in a constantly evolving space

Eddy & Eryca

The pink wall and ceiling in the living room create a fresh setting for the 1960s sofa with its original fabric, and an Aboriginal artwork by Willy Tjungurrayi titled *Tingari Dreaming*.

Eddy
&
Eryca

/

A showroom is no place to live. It is like the set of a play: dreamed up, schemed up and designed to the millimetre, a place where scripted conversation rolls out and everyone's part is clearly defined. A showroom isn't a personal space in which to be. It's no place for the tangle of layered memories and the mercurial nature of daily life.

Eddy and Eryca own and work in a furniture showroom filled with impressive pieces, but they live in a home that is so much more: a charismatic curation that tells their story. Eddy has an eagle eye for incredible vintage furniture, while Eryca—a talented photographer—has composition and colour covered. Together they run Smith Street Bazaar, a vintage store where each furniture piece and object is called out individually for its merits and its position in the timeline of significant design. Customers and other furniture dealers marvel at the couple's ability to hunt down unique pieces and often muse that their home must also be an impressive checklist of high-calibre design. It's a topic that Eryca and Eddy shy away from, finding it difficult to respond. When they walk through their home's front door after the working day, they don't see the space in terms of objects; they see it as a whole. The fact that the couple can sit in their pink-walled living room and look out to see a towering fig tree that Eddy's father planted over fifty years ago is telling: the home has meaning beyond just the stuff inside.

Eddy's Latvian father and Maltese mother met in Australia in the 1960s, and they moved into this house when Eddy was two. They planted trees, raised chickens and sheep, and made connections with the growing community around them. Eventually, Eddy moved away and started working in IT, but after winning an Art Deco bedroom suite in a darts game with friends, a passion for vintage furniture was quickly cultivated. He opened a vintage furniture store and later moved back into the family home to keep the property in the family name. Over the years, Eddy filled the house with a growing collection of furniture, an occupational hazard of being a passionate dealer. When Eryca moved in five years ago, she appreciated the history of the home and Eddy's skilful curation of furniture—but she needed to find herself in the space.

The inimitable couple, with a photograph of an owl by Gary Heery and a timber wall piece titled *Surfboard* by David Milne in the background.

The pieces in the home, both sentimental and sensationally iconic, are layered up and grouped as if in friendly conversation.

The artwork by Victor Pasmore was bought on a whim at an auction, and the brass birds are by Mexican artist Sergio Bustamante. A Bitossi owl (opposite) stands proud next to a resin vase gifted by a friend.

Whale vertebrae and 1960s glass can be found in the sitting room. The curation at the entryway (opposite) includes a photograph by Eryca, a small landscape by Emma de Clario and a colourful abstract, artist unknown.

A collection of Troika
pottery plus figurines
designed by Alexander
Girard sit on a walnut
sideboard that was made
in Melbourne by Jakob
Rudowski in the 1960s.

Eryca has been uprooted many times since she arrived in Australia as a young girl from England, so she finds the process of grounding herself in a space essential. She expresses herself with colour and thoughtfully arranges art and books around her, strengthening her connection to a location by nurturing greenery and literally putting down roots. Her philosophy of homemaking has many parallels with her photography practice. Trained in photojournalism, she focuses mainly on portraiture and creates narrative images that are deep with emotion, colour and contrast. Eryca is fascinated by the complexity of people and acknowledges the challenge of trying to capture those layers in one biographical frame. Just like an image of us that cuts to the core of who we are, she feels our homes should read as a self-portrait, layered and deeply meaningful to the individual.

Their home is confident and interesting, evolving with the seasons and creative whims. Bold hues splashed on the walls energise the rooms and bring the furniture to life. Art and decor elements, both sentimental and sensationally iconic, are layered up and grouped as if in friendly conversation. A thrift-shop figurine paid for with pocket change rests on top of a rare wall-mounted sideboard, while a cherished framed artwork by Eryca's son sits in harmony with a much sought-after Sottsass 'Planula' chair.

There is an element of irreverence in the decor, too: an oversized fibreglass dog is silhouetted by mid-morning light streaming through the linen curtains, while a taxidermy peacock stands proud on a plinth a few steps away. Whale vertebrae are piled up in the corner of a room next to a Miffy light sitting on a stack of weighty photography books. This unexpectedness lightens the mood created by some of the more significant design pieces, revealing the couple's need to not take it all so seriously.

Walk into Eryca and Eddy's showroom, and it's obvious that they have an eye for design and furniture classics; it's no wonder customers assume their home would be an extension of the showroom. Pieces from the showroom often spend time in their home, and vice versa, but the complete biography of Eryca, Eddy and their home is bigger than individual pieces: it's layered and constantly evolving. The house has undergone two renovations since the 1960s, and the couple is drafting plans for the third, keen to reinvent the space while keeping its history intact. They could move away and start anew, but the connections to the layers of this house are just too strong.

Eryca found the silk curtains (left) and vintage paintings (opposite) in thrift shops. A small, framed photo by Bill Henson is shown below, along with figures from Italy and ancient India.

In the master bedroom,
Eryca has hung a set of
Japanese prints that she
bought in a thrift shop; the
team of horses (opposite)
was found on the side of
the road.

New to you: living with vintage + antiques

Do you get a little thrill when you come across magnificent vintage items? I grew up in a home that was, and still is, filled with pre-loved furniture pieces. Family heirlooms sat next to side-of-the-road finds that had been restored by my dad; rarely, if ever, did anything get delivered, box-fresh, from a furniture store. Weekends were spent on a well-trodden route of antique and old-ware emporiums, trash and treasure markets and thrift shops, and each day's adventure began with a ritualistic circling of the garage-sale listings in the local paper.

These weekends taught me about thriftiness and the alternatives to the big-name retailers. My taste for interesting pieces was formed (or is it genetic?), and I grew to appreciate items with a backstory and a sense of history. I learned to look out for the cues of a well-made piece—makers' marks, signs of the handmade as well as construction techniques from years gone by.

The tour of my own home on pages 238–51, however, will show you that I don't entirely shun the new. Looking around my home office as I type this, I will confess that the majority of the furniture in this room arrived as flat packs, with an allen key drowning in a hugely intimidating sachet of screws and washers. The pieces do the trick of holding my stuff, but that's about it—they are purely functional, and I have no emotional attachment to them. There is no romantic backstory, and feelings of the past aren't evoked when I look at the shiny white pieces.

My office chair, however, has its own biography. I saw it on a Facebook marketplace page and was drawn to the shape of the seat and the solid swivel leg. The yellowing label underneath tells me that it was manufactured by Pongrass Furniture, an Australian company that was producing chairs in the 1960s and 1970s. Besides being incredibly comfortable and well made, the chair connects me to Australia's history; I can't help but imagine the sorts of rooms this solid furniture piece has seen since its production in the mid-twentieth century. In a room that is already busily humming with props, images and ideas, this chair gives my office a certain energy and a sense of connectedness to other times and lives.

Old pieces are reassuring, and they symbolise steadiness. They have worked their way through the generations—integrated into the daily lives of a cast of characters—and have stood the test of time. The way we shop for old pieces also represents the 'slow decorating' approach to making a home. Instead of purchasing the entirety of a living room in one mindless transaction during a dizzying Saturday in a showroom, buying vintage means that you have to wait it out until the ideal piece crosses your path. So many vintage lovers I've met effuse about the thrill of the hunt and the immense satisfaction in finding the perfect piece after months, or even years, of searching. It makes the piece all the more valuable.

Old pieces also represent an environmentally friendly way of making a home. Not only are you saving a piece from ending up in landfill, but you are also minimising the nasty VOCs (volatile organic compounds) that the cheap, mass-produced new pieces will emit into your home's air via the synthetic materials used in manufacturing. Even if your vintage piece is made of synthetic materials, the VOCs would have long dissipated by the time the item is introduced into your home.

For me, the scent of dusty timber and a lingering sense of the past will always trump shiny and new.

Top tips for acquiring 'new to you' pieces

▶ Be persistent and consistent. Visit thrift shops, markets, vintage and antique retailers, junk shops and online marketplaces whenever you can—you never know when that perfect-for-you piece will surface.

▶ Get educated and price savvy. It's good to know when something is fairly priced or incorrectly tagged as authentic vintage. Ask the seller questions, and research any visible manufacturer names for price comparisons. Look out for labels and makers' marks, or request photos of these if shopping online.

▶ Don't be afraid of surface scratches. These can often be buffed out with the right furniture oil, and sometimes a little wear and tear gives a piece character anyway. Don't worry about wobbly legs, either—often a simple tightening of the screws will steady furniture items.

▶ Ignore seat coverings. Look beyond the dated or damaged upholstery, and check out the bones of the piece. Investment in reupholstering will give the item a whole new lease on life.

▶ Seek out real wood. In my mind, solid timber wins out over particleboard every time.

▶ Good things come to those who wait. Keep a checklist of the items you are looking for (and the measurements required), and jump on something if it pops up. Who knows when you will see that piece again?

A historical cottage thoughtfully preserved

Sarah & Phil

The colours in the artwork (below) by Sarah Webb's cousin, Ellie Jansson, echo the cool blues and greens of the stunning views from Thorne Cottage looking out beyond the exterior entertaining area (opposite).

Sarah
&
Phil

The story of Thorne Cottage starts with the First Fleet, and for Tasmanian natives Sarah and Phil, the couple who live in the seaside cottage, it is a story that reveals itself a little more each day. The couple often answers the door to descendants of the family who lived in Thorne during the 1800s, and digging on the property uncovers china and glass pieces from the past. Life in the cottage today can't be separated from how life used to be, but Sarah and Phil are finding their own way to live with the history of Thorne.

Sarah is a ceramicist whose work has a sense of nostalgia set into it, directly influenced by Thorne Cottage. Phil works in IT and has always taken a special interest in Tasmanian heritage homes and stories of the past. It was Phil who spotted Thorne Cottage on the market and urged Sarah to take a chance on it, asking her to look past the timber-laminate panelling and dusty carpets that covered all surfaces, the residue of an unsympathetic update during the 1970s. She also had to look past the damp spongy walls, the crumbling windowsills and the barely functioning kitchen and bathroom, and instead focus on the few glimmers of charm among the dreariness. Tall ceilings feature in the main living areas, and the original marble fireplace stands firm. Solid floorboards dip with the tread of residents from centuries past. The cottage is situated on a large corner block, allowing space for an expansive vegie garden and a roomy ceramic studio, with a spectacular outlook towards sparkling Clarks Bay, east of Hobart.

One day, Sarah and Phil were digging trenches in the front yard to sort out the drainage when a busload of schoolkids piled out in front and proceeded to have a history lesson covering the significance of the home and its place in Tasmanian history. The couple knew that the cottage was old, but until that point they had had no idea how historically significant it was. The sandstone cottage was a family home built in the 1820s by a Royal Marine Sergeant who came to Australia on the First Fleet. It later operated as an inn and was a rest stop for thirsty soldiers who were happy to lock their convicts in Thorne's cellar while they enjoyed an ale upstairs before continuing on to Port Arthur.

Sarah and Phil Webb love to host guests in their sandstone ruin, a recent outdoor addition that gives the couple space to entertain.

Tilba, seen at right with Sarah, and Milton knock the furniture with their tails as they bound through the house. Tall ceilings downstairs and ornate details (opposite) lend a sense of grandeur to the small rooms.

The cottage was eventually taken over by a large family with 13 children who continued to live in it for many generations. The descendants of that large family occasionally knock on Thorne's door with fascinating pictures and stories of the past, reminding Sarah and Phil of the home's history and pulling them back into life as it once was.

Sarah and Phil consider themselves custodians of Thorne Cottage. They've worked with skilled builders who honoured the age of the building, restoring and preserving the convict-era architectural features where possible. The internal staircase had been stripped of all detail in the 1970s, so the couple worked with a craftsman to reinstate a design closer to the original. They recently hired a stonemason to help build a sandstone outdoor room, designed to look like a tumbled-down building in the style of Thorne Cottage. The couple uses the relaxed space they affectionately call 'the ruin' to host gatherings of friends and family, something that is near impossible in the tight rooms of Thorne. Kids rumble in the lush vegetable garden while the outdoor pizza oven bakes away; the couple's happy dogs, Tilba and Milton, perch by the long timber table in the hope of catching dropped food.

Look closely at the walls of the ruin, and you will see fragments of pottery and pieces of stamped glass wedged in between the sandstone blocks. These are the relics of Thorne's past, the reminders that reveal themselves whenever the couple digs on the property or heavy rains swamp the land. In collecting the fragments and incorporating them into the next stages of the home, Phil and Sarah are archiving the history of Thorne in their own way. Sarah also uses the fragments to inspire the designs of her ceramic pieces, giving her range the sense of old-world charm for which the work is renowned. She has always been a maker, but it was the move into the cottage that really helped her find her direction. She had never been a fan of living in old homes, but Thorne Cottage has won her over.

The home is suitably dressed with precious antiques that Phil has inherited and old wares that Sarah has uncovered at markets and garage sales. Besides a handful of modern things, such as the flashy coffee machine in the kitchen, Phil's beast of a motorcycle in the garage and the sound of contemporary music that filters through the rooms, you feel as if time hasn't passed in Thorne. Sarah and Phil know that they have the opportunity to keep the stories of Thorne Cottage alive and have found a way not only to build their own memories into it but also to share it with others.

Sarah and Phil know that they have the opportunity to keep the stories of Thorne Cottage alive, and they have found their own way to do it.

Sarah's ceramic studio sits beside Thorne Cottage. Her designs are inspired by the delicate patterns found on the many china fragments uncovered on the grounds.

The beauty of
old homes

—

Do you celebrate the cracks and quirks of vintage homes? If so, I salute you. To the businesses and individuals who are hell-bent on erasing old homes and building bland, cheap, soulless boxes in their place, PLEASE STOP! We need to preserve and appreciate the structures that connect us to our past, as individuals and as a society. On page 42, I talk about how vintage furniture pieces are reassuring, as their existence through the generations signifies a steadiness and permanence. Old buildings have the same anchoring effect; a well-built structure filled with original character reminds us of where we have come from. It tunes us into the way life used to be, giving us a point of reference that forces us to put our own life into perspective. It's humbling.

You can sum up the aesthetic appeal of a vintage home with a list of its architectural details, as evidence of skilled craftsmanship and the home's place in the history of design: the handsome timber fretwork and leadlight glass in Federation-era homes, the sunken living rooms of mid-century houses, the ornate plasterwork of the Victorian era and so on. These elements are the tangible connection to the past, the visual signifiers that texturise the space and heighten the senses. But there is also something intangible that draws us into vintage homes. Design features can be replicated and it's always wonderful to see them done well, but it's the soul and romance of an old home that can never be fully manufactured. I don't believe in ghosts, but I do believe that vintage homes have a spirit that grows stronger over decades of human contact.

Homes age just as humans do; as the years push on, more upkeep is required. Things start to sag, they get a bit weatherworn, and a single issue can lead to a string of complications. It's true that restoring an older home can be costly, and even more so if the building is historically significant (your local council will be able to advise you if this is the case). If your home is heritage-listed, discussion will turn to 'renovation versus restoration versus preservation', and you will need to enlist specialist architects and contractors to navigate the design and building restrictions. Dedicated and passionate people forge ahead with these sorts of projects (it's not for everyone!), and their hard work contributes to the understanding of our country's history, an invaluable outcome that benefits us all.

When I eventually update my own home (we could do with more room in the kitchen), I don't want to lose the feeling of warmth it exudes or the 1970s-era details. Any updates will be in keeping with the home's style and will be sympathetic to the history of the building. Even though the building isn't historically significant according to the council, the house has been sitting on the block for over forty years; it was built to last, and it deserves this position for many decades to come.

Thank you to the champions of vintage homes. It makes me happy to hear about people who respect the past and see value in keeping old houses alive for future generations to admire, to learn from and to live in. If you dream of living in an older home with character, but your current home lacks the layers of detail, or if you are designing a new home and want to give it an old-world twist, there are plenty of decorating ideas you can try.

Ten ways to bring vintage charm to your spaces

1 Decorate with worn timber furniture and threadbare oriental rugs—the more texture, the better.

2 Swap contemporary light fittings for appealing designs from (or inspired by) the mid-century and earlier.

3 Use leather, brass, linen and any other materials that age beautifully.

4 Stay away from anything that has a faux distressed finish—it's too contrived and won't feel authentic.

5 Add wall mouldings, picture rails, wooden panelling or ornate skirting.

6 Replace contemporary doors with reclaimed timber styles.

7 Update your modern hardware with handles, knobs and drawer pulls that feature interesting details and naturally aged finishes.

8 Visit a building-salvage yard to look for cool architectural elements such as old window frames, timber mantles and banged-up signs, and display them in your home as if they are sculptures.

9 Use wallpaper to add depth to a room, and choose a pattern that hints at bygone eras.

10 If your TV is mounted on the wall, pull it down immediately and hide it in a cupboard!

Light and
colour in a
home among
the trees

/

Cassy, Gil,
Ivy & Gypsy

There is a never-ending rotation of art, knick-knacks and furniture, but the feeling of a perfectly functioning space remains.

The kitchen works well for the family; the cook stays on one side of the island bench, and onlookers stick to the other side. The double doors to the backyard open up the space.

Cassy, Gil,
Ivy & Gypsy

/

A coffee table brought Cassy and me together. The keen thrift shopper, and long-time resident of my neighbourhood, had listed the tile-topped piece on a local online marketplace, an activity she often does to keep her house decluttered and her collections under control. The coffee table was being replaced with one of Cassy's recent highly prized finds—a table with a terrarium in its glass-domed undercarriage, filled with plastic plants and stale air from the 1970s.

After skipping over to Cassy's house and being cheerfully greeted at the front door of the white weatherboard home perched on the high side of the street, I stepped into the three-bedroom cottage and said the thing that most people say when they first visit Cassy's house: 'I can see right into your bathroom!' The internal wall in between the living space and the en suite bathroom is made up of glass panels, which means that the toilet and the raised claw-foot tub are in full sight of the living room and front door. It's unexpected, but for Cassy, husband Gil and their young girls, Ivy and Gypsy, it's no big deal. This is their home; it is a private space that they comfortably share with each other.

The house is vibrant with colour, pattern and a never-ending rotation of art, knick-knacks and furniture pieces. Storage space is limited in the home and the bedrooms are petite, hence Cassy's discipline with her collections, but the idea of upsizing doesn't make sense to her and Gil. The home in which they have raised their family has functioned perfectly for them over the years and continues to do so as Ivy and Gypsy grow up.

The small space brings them together, but each family member will retreat to their own corner, to work on their own thing, when a time-out is needed. Gil, who works in publishing, has set up a gym in a room under the house, while Cassy, currently building on her ceramics practice, has a studio space in a nearby suburb. Little Ivy, despite her sweet demeanour, is a fiercely talented and competitive mountain-bike rider with a strict training schedule, and level-headed Gypsy is an eager reader who also takes acting lessons in the city. If anyone feels too cooped up, the expanse of the national park is at their back doorstep and the waterfront is just one street away.

The four members of the family—along with their rescue dog, Tiggy—are drawn to the light in this part of the house.

Cassy Gilbert covered the living room wall with wallpaper she found in her parents' attic. The matching lampshade came three years later, a serendipitous side-of-the-road find.

A retro terrarium coffee table is filled with its original faux plants, while the new sofa is layered with cushions made from vintage Finnish fabric.

A Fler dining chair, awaiting new upholstery, sits next to a stunning second-hand china cabinet in a corner by the kitchen.

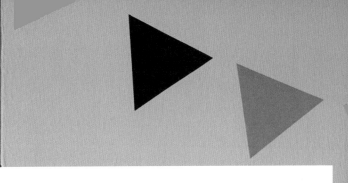

When Cassy bought the house at the turn of the millennium, before she met Gil, it was the water views and green surrounds that pulled her in. Her friends thought she was crazy to give up her inner-city life and move an hour away to a tiny, isolated town, but for Cassy it was a much-needed shift to a quieter life among the trees and by the ocean, with a stronger connection to nature. The house, one of the original shacks in the bay, was made up of dark, poky rooms, and the front verandah was covered in tattered lattice left over from the 1980s. Cassy moved in and, over the course of six years, the cottage was updated with more windows, glass-panelled doors and bigger rooms. The verandah was enclosed with large windows, which expanded the living-room footprint. The kitchen was extended, the backyard decking was put in place and the en suite was installed.

If the wall between the en suite and the living room wasn't made of glass panels, both rooms would feel boxy and the incredible light that comes through this aspect of the north-facing house would be lost. Each family member is drawn to the dining table that sits next to the front windows, and a variety of activities play out in this space. The table is the place for meals, for homework and paperwork, for art and craft; it's the hub of the home, bathed in light and freshened with sea breezes. Here, the light shifts over the course of the day, hitting the stained-glass windows in the en suite and bouncing off the mirrors, making the family feel as if they are in an old-school kaleidoscope. The bath sits on a platform that is elevated to the perfect height for watching the sailboats bob across the bay, and it is positioned so that you can soak in the sun as you soak in the tub. Cassy has no regrets or apologies about opening up the en suite to the living space, as the pay-off is too great. When guests do visit, they can always use the other bathroom located off the kitchen and close the door behind them.

I often see Cassy, Gil and the girls out and about in our neighbourhood, riding bikes or swimming off the jetty. Cassy and I catch up and share our latest thrift-shop finds, as she, like me, is addicted to the thrill of the hunt and is the kind of persistent shopper who reaps the rewards of never walking past a second-hand store without doing a quick scan of the shelves. For this book, the photography of Cassy and Gil's home occurred over two sessions, with quite a few months' gap in between. It was no surprise that in that time, new artwork had been put in place and rugs and decor had been switched up. Little things had shifted but, overall, the feeling of a perfectly functioning space remained.

11/11/16 →

Stained-glass windows in the en suite look out to the water (opposite), while the panelled glass above the sinks views the living space. A detail from the girls' bedroom (below) shows vintage artworks and pretty bunting.

Live with children without losing your own style

———

Hands up if, when prepping your home for the arrival of your first baby, you bought a new easy-care leather sofa, you had all the carpet ripped up and replaced with hardwood timber, and you repainted every single wall with stain-resistant paint? Anyone? No? A quick skim of articles about 'styling your home in a child-friendly way' will have you believe that money and messy renovations are the answer to getting your house baby-ready—a bitter pill to swallow when you may be struggling to accept that life as you know it is about to become a foggy memory. I am yet to step onto the roller-coaster ride called parenting, but I am in awe of the sacrifices that parents make across all segments of life when two become three.

I have observed the many ways—the good, the bad and the outright chaotic—that home life has changed for family members and friends of mine who have launched into parenthood. Days are filled with tears, smells and spills, and a tsunami of toys and tiny clothes rolls through rooms relentlessly. The purpose of the home often shifts. It can become a workplace—and, indeed, a parent's whole world for a while—especially if the primary carer needs to juggle work responsibilities with looking after an infant. There is also a new angle of functionality and safety that needs to be considered.

The pressure is on to create a perfectly nurturing environment for your child, but the idea of living in a home that looks like a preschool will likely make you want to hide under a pile of unwashed laundry. Even though your life is about to be turned upside down, it doesn't mean your home has to completely flip as well. Your own sense of style can continue to shine through, the finances don't have to take a huge hit, and your little one can still contently giggle away in a warm, supportive home.

Parenthood is filled with compromises, but you don't have to give up your individual sense of style.

Ways to find a happy balance in your nest

Storage

For the youngsters I know, the amount of stuff they have acquired is not at all proportional to the amount of time they have been on the planet—where does it all come from?* Floors and tabletops disappear under never-ending waves of stuff, and rogue pieces turn up in the strangest of places. Bulky plastic tubs are practical and definitely have their place, but there are many other more aesthetically pleasing storage options available that will look good sitting in the corner of the room. You could go with woven baskets, ply crates or a vintage trunk, checking first that they are child-friendly.

* I'm looking at you, Grandma and Grandpa!

Wall colours

Countless articles wax on about the latest trending colour in children's rooms or how a gender-neutral scheme is the only way to go. I would hate to think that there are parents out there who feel bad because they haven't painted their nursery or kid's room in a carefully chosen colour; it's not necessary. Let the existing colour scheme in the house flow into the kid's room.

Many of us already have some variation of white on our walls, and it's a perfect blank slate for a room that needs to easily adapt to the stages of growth your little one is about to shoot through. The only situation where I would look to repaint the walls is if the existing paint is high-intensity red or orange—energising colours like these will keep your child wide-eyed and buzzed, making a big mess of already nebulous sleeping patterns.

Art

Artworks on your walls is a visual reminder that you are still an adult with grown-up interests and tastes, even if you do spend most of your day negotiating with a toddler! Art adds colour, texture and a bit of polish to a space and, as it usually sits up high, it is out of the reach of inquisitive little hands. A big artwork in your living room makes a statement and can distract your guests from the toys and books scattered across the floor. It's kind of equivalent to slapping on some lipstick when you haven't had time to properly do your hair … this actually might be another trick that gets you through those really tough days!

Objects

When your child kicks off into their wobbly first step, you will most likely need to relocate any of your favourite objects and treasured collections that are displayed at a low height. However, it doesn't mean that every surface area from the hip down has to be stark and decoration-free for the next six years. Once your child gains confidence in their motor skills, reintroduce the items for a wonderful learning opportunity about respect for others' personal belongings and the value of an interesting home. If children can learn to be careful with smaller items, hopefully they will apply that level of care to everything in the house. Interacting with objects of different textures, shapes and weights can help build cognitive processes and instil a sense of curiosity in a child. Anything of extreme value may have to live up higher for a little longer and, of course, you must make sure all objects are kid-friendly, but the goal overall is to share with your child the things that are meaningful to you.

A magical
retreat inspired
by the sea

Sarah

Sarah

Sit with Sarah in the waterside cottage she calls Captain's Rest, and you get an immediate sense that the space she has created is a pure and honest reflection of what she needs in life. Sarah's part-time home, the cottage nestles into a cluster of shacks that overlooks the ethereal Lettes Bay, with the Tasmanian Wilderness World Heritage Area beyond. A jetty juts out into the water just a few steps from Sarah's front door, and the area's history swims and swirls through the misty atmosphere. The beauty of the cottage cannot be separated from the majesty of the natural world that surrounds it, and both are Sarah's bulwarks against hard times.

A sea captain at heart and an adventurer to her core, Sarah's past is a patchwork of travelling the world and chasing the endlessness of the ocean. After almost a decade of crisscrossing the globe, she bought a 1970s sailing boat in California with the intention of sailing solo back to Australia. One night, off the coast of Mexico, the rough seas forced her to stop. Around 1 am, the boat hit something deep below (a sleeping whale, perhaps?), and water came gushing in. Sarah clung desperately to the deck as the sea smashed the hull apart and the boat crumbled. The Mexican Navy eventually pulled her out of the ocean, but they were unable to salvage the boat or any of her belongings. Without a stitch to her name, her passport and identification washed away, Sarah spent six months stranded in a Mexican village awaiting consular assistance, living in a coastal shack and helped by the friendly locals.

When Sarah finally returned home to Western Australia, her priorities had shifted; the near-death experience on the sea and daily life in the rudimentary shack had rebooted her. She had come to love the sense of simplicity and anonymity that the shack had given her, and she knew that getting grounded somewhere beautiful and remote was key to her happiness.

Sarah had heard about the mysteriousness of the Tasmanian wilderness, and when she spotted what was to become her cottage in a magazine, she knew that Lettes Bay—located on the west coast—would give her exactly what she was looking for.

Captain's Rest is Sarah Andrews' grounding place and where her heart is anchored, despite the fact that she only lives here part-time.

Sarah feels secure and protected in this corner, under the watchful eye of the characters in her vintage paintings and surrounded by velvet cushions that were sewn by her parents.

The cottage is decorated with objects and materials found locally, including washed-up ropes and coral; timber from the neighbour's scrap pile became the kitchen benchtop (opposite).

The salvaged windows, stamped with an 1800s date and painstakingly restored by Sarah over six weeks, frame the magical view of the bay.

Reading further into the history of the area, Sarah learned that the cluster of cottages had been the place for grieving families to heal and recuperate after losing loved ones in a tragic local mining accident that had occurred in the early 1900s. The west coast of Tasmania is known for its rugged and unforgiving landscapes, and as the location of Australia's most hellish penal colony in the convict era, but there is a feeling of restoration and quiet contemplation that seems to permeate the still cove of Lettes Bay.

While the views out of the cottage's windows are captivating, the interiors are equally as intoxicating. It took six months for Sarah and a builder to reconfigure the original run-down cottage. She designed the space herself, knowing that large windows to capture the expanse of the view were a priority, as were multiple spots to sit and lounge. Her experience with boats and the design of small but functional spaces influenced her approach to the build; clever built-in seating with hidden storage makes the most of the cottage's small footprint, as do the narrow doorways.

The cottage is decorated in a thoughtful way, inspired by seafaring adventures and an old-world aesthetic with a romantic hue. Characters of the past peer out from canvases dotted throughout the cottage, foraged natural elements and patinated finishes add texture to vignettes, while layers of linen, velvet and animal hides feel good to touch. Rich and spicy scented candles flicker, adding a veil of giddiness to the total sensory experience of the small space.

Sarah is an entrepreneurial creative who works as a stylist and travels often, so when she isn't at Captain's Rest, she shares the space with others; the cottage is a sought-after holiday rental for people wanting a slice of romance and respite. When Sarah is at Captain's Rest, she spends her hours soaking in the claw-foot tub and then lying on the window seat, buffered by plump cushions, looking out to the jetty and beyond.

Drawing and poring over boating maps and charts is done at the desk nook. Come dinnertime, Sarah glides her timber rowboat across the inky water to check her nets for fat salmon. The only sounds are the birds and the daily toot-toot from the steam train that runs through the ancient trees on the other side of the bay, another signifier of the area's past. Sarah feels most like herself when she is here. She lets her hair go wild, and she uses the quiet time to take note of her breathing, to observe the mist as it rolls through and to catch the daily rainbows that kiss the waterline.

Canvas and rope are the materials of Sarah's seafaring adventures, while bare feet and cooking on outdoor fires typify her time on the land at Captain's Rest. The bedroom (opposite) is cosy with linen, velvet and a stack of books always at the ready.

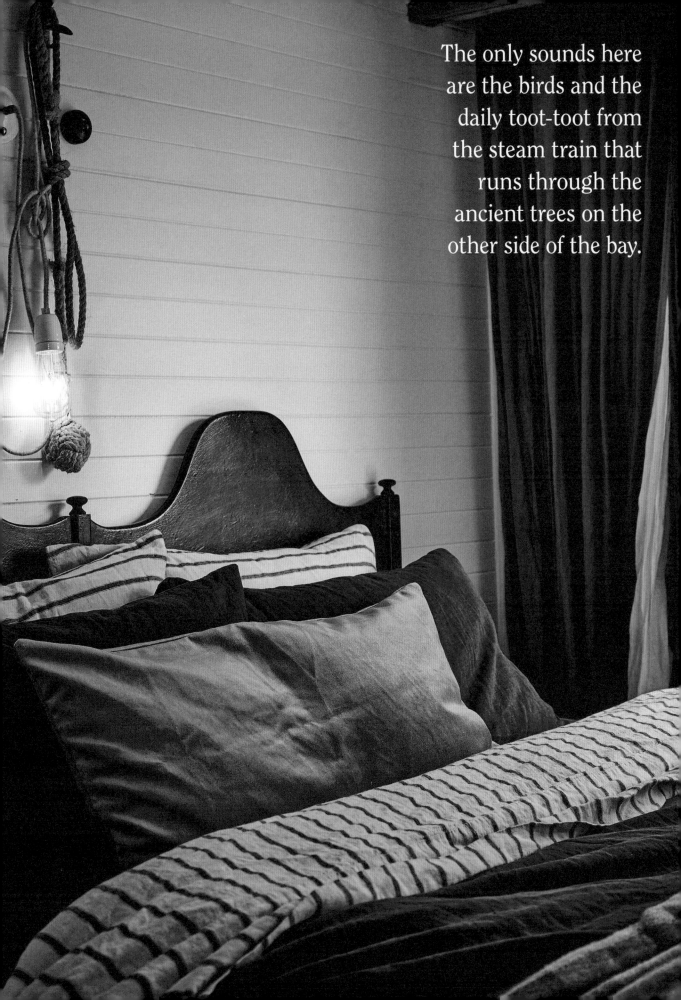

The only sounds here are the birds and the daily toot-toot from the steam train that runs through the ancient trees on the other side of the bay.

How to balance function and style in a small space

As much as I love the idea of wide-open rooms that roll through a home and spill out onto a sprawling backyard, there is definite appeal in the intimacy of a smaller space. Instead of rattling around in a too-big home, people are brought together in small spaces and social interactions are fostered. Energy bills can potentially be reduced when the footprint of the space is condensed, and it takes less stuff to furnish a petite space. And do you know what less floor space also means? Less vacuuming! That sounds great, eh?

However, living in small spaces definitely comes with a cache of frustrations. Perhaps you live in a squished apartment, or your living room feels too cramped. How does that make you feel? It's tricky to find the balance between function and style in a space where there's barely enough room to open a newspaper. You want to simplify the space but not strip it completely of your story. A sharp edit of items is needed, drilling down to carefully selected furniture pieces that have purpose.

A small space can quickly become chaotic and overwhelming if it lacks organisation and is too cluttered. You will find yourself avoiding the space and the uneasy feeling it brings, and your relationship with your home overall will feel disconnected. The goal is to make the small space functional without compromising on your own personal style.

A small space can quickly become chaotic and overwhelming if it lacks organisation.

Solve your small-space dilemma

The edit

Define the purpose of the space and subtract the furniture items that have no use. Make the space fully functional by arranging the essential items only. Don't feel that you have to downsize all your furniture to match the scale of the room, either—no one wants to live in a doll's house! The trick is to be selective with the larger hero items you add to a space, and limit your choice to only one or two bigger pieces. Make a note of the way everyone navigates the space, and rearrange the pieces to create clear pathways and a natural, easy flow of foot traffic.

A small space bulging with knick-knacks will feel cluttered and overwhelming. You can still layer up the space with loved items and artworks, but resist the urge to place an item on every surface. By balancing the busier areas with clean, clear spaces, your special pieces will stand out and the room will feel calmer overall.

The storage

You need to squeeze in the storage opportunities wherever you can when space is limited. This could mean something as simple as choosing a coffee table that has drawers underneath, or it could involve a design solution such as a custom-built window seat that opens up to store extra blankets and cushions. It's important that everything has a home and is returned to that spot after use if you want to keep on top of the organisation and cleanliness.

Make the most of the available wall space by affixing floating shelves, wall-mounted cabinets or a fold-out table that could double as a desk or benchtop. By getting furniture up off the floor, you free up valuable real estate and open up the options for more storage under wall-mounted pieces.

The illusions

The easiest way to create the illusion of more space in the room is to paint the walls a shade of white and stick to lighter tones for the flooring and furniture. Natural light will bounce around the white surfaces like a ping-pong ball, even more so if you add mirrors or mirrored furniture. Conversely, it is interesting to think about what dark, moody hues and finishes can do for a small space. For instance, inky indigo walls will create a sense of infinity, as edges of the space push out and the room's depth appears to continue. If you like the idea of making a bold statement with your small space, this dramatic approach could be the answer for you. Bonus impact points are given if you are brave enough to paint your ceiling in the same dark hue as your walls!

Whether you go with light or dark on your walls and floors, you need to consider how contrasting colour affects the illusion of openness and continuation. To use an example from the world of fashion: think about how nude-coloured high heels give the illusion of a longer leg, whereas black high heels cap off the leg length at the ankle and act like a full stop. If you have lighter walls and floors, go with furniture in lighter colours, and the same principle applies to our friends who turn to the dark side—choose darker furniture pieces to avoid contrasts that disrupt that sense of infinity.

If you are blessed with tall ceilings, highlight the vertical space in the room and draw the eye up by arranging art on the walls or suspending a hanging plant or two. Installing curtains that drop from well above the window frame will also exaggerate the room's height and impart a sense of grandeur.

A wonky
home,
handmade
with love

Annie,
Genevieve,
Olive & Oscar

Perched on a hill, the home
was made entirely out of
reclaimed materials and
hand-built by the family,
with the assistance of
loved ones.

Annie, Genevieve, Olive & Oscar

Annie, Genevieve and their two kids, Olive and Oscar, have lived in southern New South Wales on Autumn Farm for seven years. In that time, they have hand-built two homes on the 2.8-hectare plot (one tiny home and one not so tiny), run a pastured chicken farm, beat cancer and formed a tight-knit community around them. Fingers, big and small, are never still in this household. Masses of produce have been grown and harvested, and every meal is lovingly made from scratch. Crafty projects keep Olive and Oscar off their screens, and the whole family lives by a DIY ethic, finding happiness in sharing their creations with others.

For the first five years on the land, the family lived in a 26-square-metre straw-bale home they built themselves, along with the help of supportive friends and family. The tiny home included one open-plan room and a sleeping loft, with the kitchen, bathroom and dining area outdoors. Coming from the gritty inner west of Sydney, the family quickly took to spending their home time outdoors and working on the land. A bountiful fruit and vegetable garden was established, and everyone embraced the daily task of tending to their growing menagerie.

The family positioned themselves in the local food network, building the connections for bartering and, more importantly, solid friendships and support. During their time in the tiny house, Annie was diagnosed with breast cancer and underwent a series of harsh chemo treatments after a mastectomy. She slowly recovered in the sunshine, and nourished her body with clean, organic food grown on their land or dropped off by neighbours, and prepared by Gen. Not one to sit idle, Annie maintained a fierce determination to get back into action. With cancer behind them, the family broke ground to make way for their 'big house', a 93-square-metre, off-grid, passive-solar, straw-bale building.

The tiny house had taught them vital lessons in the technical aspects of hand-building a structure, but living in the space altered their view of what they thought they needed to be happy. The original plans for the big house included larger bedrooms, but that idea shifted when they realised that communal areas—where they could cook, craft and read together—were more important.

The close-knit family members, with their two dogs, Sock and Shine, love their rural life and the community around them.

After five years of cooking on a camp stove in the tiny house, Gen Derwent was elated to move into the big kitchen. Annie Werner stripped the paint off the chest of drawers (opposite) and replaced the knobs.

The whole family agrees
that the way the morning
sun turns everything
golden is magical. The
recycled timber table was
made by Annie for Gen.

Fingers big and small
are never still in this
household that lives
by a DIY ethic.

Annie cherishes the
woodcut that belonged
to her Oma when she was
a little girl (above). Flowers
picked in their rambling
garden add more colour
to the home.

The ritual of bathing outdoors was established during their time in the tiny house, centred on fire baths in an old metal tub Annie found at the tip and nestled into the land. The family came to love the calming act of filling the bath with the garden hose, lighting a fire underneath the tub and then luxuriating in a soak, taking in the view of the spring-fed dam at the bottom of the property. The plans for a completely internal bathroom in the big house were scrapped, and the fire bath was reinstated. It is now sitting by a greenhouse that contains a shower and a dry toilet, still with a stunning vista across the valley.

A roomy kitchen and dining space was always at the centre of the blueprints for the big house, a pure joy for Gen, who loves to cook and host gatherings. The home includes a temperature-regulated walk-in pantry, the same size as the bedrooms, indicating just how seriously these ladies take their food preparation and storage. Pickling, fermenting, preserving and curing are constantly happening in the background, and every dish served at the generous 18-seat dining table is garnished with even more homemade tastiness. Annie built the 4.5-metre table using old fence palings and bridge timbers, and the happy collection of chairs pulled up to the table's perimeter were gathered from junk stores and the tip. Now, when friends and family drop in—which is a welcome and regular occurrence—there is always space to pull up an extra plate, a mismatched chair and a hand-sewn napkin.

Dinnertime is an important part of the family's routine. During the meal, the family members take turns listing the things that made them happy that day, a practice of gratitude that helps everyone stay focused on the positive. Olive and Oscar attend the local school, and Annie and Gen hold off-farm jobs that keep them busy outside of the hours they put into their crops and their animals. They have worked hard to build up this lifestyle around them, nurturing a way of life that is an authentic reflection of their values. Their happy home on Autumn Farm is a daily reminder that, with perseverance and a support network, anything can be achieved and it will be all the more rewarding. It is a wonky home, handmade with love.

Rituals at Autumn Farm include bathing outdoors in the fire bath, and rising early to feed the ducks and chickens. Annie's resourceful mum found the salvaged pink sink that now sits in the greenhouse bathroom (opposite).

How to harness the happiness of handmade

——

Have you ever spent time making a handmade gift for a loved one? Or, for the craft-klutzes out there, have you ever received a present that had been lovingly made especially for you? It's a warm and fuzzy experience. A homemade card tucked into a hand-knitted scarf represents a whole lot of love and thought—that handmade item has a value beyond just the cost of the materials. The idea that each object—complete with the metaphorical (and sometimes literal) fingerprint of the maker—is unique and can never be replicated infuses the item with significance. The time it takes for someone to make something also adds value to an item, especially in our busy modern-day world where speed and convenience are the norm. When the world is whirling around us, it's nice to stop and think about the pure act of hands touching raw material and creating.

The heart and hand work together as we get lost in the motions of creating something out of nothing; making is good for our wellbeing. Troubled thoughts are distracted during the process, and it's hard to beat the sense of accomplishment that fills your soul as you step back to observe your completed project. As I type this, sitting on my desk in front of me is a ceramic dish I made at a workshop on a sunny Saturday afternoon last year. The dish is filled with paper clips and Post-It Notes, and to say the piece is 'imperfect' would be an understatement! But when I look at the dish, I see beyond the dodgy edges and muddy glaze—instead, I am reminded of the feel of the cool clay as I formed the dish shape; I can see my hands painting the wobbly lines. The experience of the workshop comes back to me, and I think about how it was a worthy way to spend my time, learning from passionate people and getting my hands dirty. Looking at the corralled stationary on my desk wouldn't induce in me the same positive emotions if the bits were contained in a mass-produced, store-bought dish.

Even if we aren't decorating our homes entirely with items made especially for us or by us, we can make conscious decisions to choose handmade products over mass-produced items. Just as second-hand furniture is imbued with stories of the past, a handmade item is infused with the energy of the maker. Regardless of whether the maker is a venerated artisan or the yet-to-be-discovered art genius/toddler in your family, the piece they make will hum with meaning and their presence. You cannot separate a handmade item from the person who made it. We bring soul into our homes when we decorate with things that have been shaped, knitted, knotted, printed and painted by human hands.

A handmade item is infused with
the energy of the maker.

Handy homespun hints

At the core of the handmade concept is a connection with others. Here are some ideas on how to enrich your life with more handmade items.

◢ Enrol in an art workshop or short craft course, and allow for time to experiment. Don't be hard on yourself if you think that what you make isn't any good—enjoy the experience of learning with others and be proud of whatever it is you produce. Frame your painting or photo, and use that coffee mug daily.

◢ Take advantage of 'open studio' days. Go into the creative spaces of artists and makers to learn more about their process and the energy that goes into their work.

◢ Shop at handmade markets, and support your local creative talent.

◢ Make art and craft with the youngsters in your family. Out of the mess will come something beautiful, as whatever is created represents the time you and the little ones spent together.

◢ Reach out to friends and family members who create and make, and ask them to give you a demonstration. You never know what newly acquired skill, or collaborative partnership, may come out of it.

◢ If you want to start giving handmade presents but are overwhelmed by the idea of it, a gesture as small as making your own gift tags to add to your store-bought presents won't go unnoticed.

Retro style and
room to breathe
in a spacious
split-level home

Dann, Arron,
Molly & Lola

Arron Fletcher and the family's cat, Seamus, often fight over who gets to sit in the green chair. A space dedicated to Arron's music overlooks the living room.

Dann, Arron,
Molly & Lola

The 1960s were a heady swirl of wailing guitars, passionate protests and groovy gurus. The times were changing, and many people latched onto Eastern practices of meditation to help transcend the helter-skelter of the world. While Dann doesn't chant mantras or follow Eastern philosophies, she does subscribe to her own form of meditation, a therapeutic practice that helped her through a rough patch in the past and continues to fill her with a sense of calm today.

Dann's peace comes in the form of hunting down retro homewares and the act of puttering around the house. The sound of the word 'puttering' implies that this activity is meaningless but, for Dann, arranging things 'just so' relaxes her. The large home she and her family rent is a vibrant tribute to the 1960s and 1970s, a skilfully curated time warp that offers the whole family happiness with its proximity to the beach, views of a green escarpment and plenty of space for their cat, Seamus, to caper about.

To take one step into the sprawling, split-level home is to understand that a serious collector lives here. Macramé owls and Donald Clark wall-hangings feature en masse, and a rainbow of Italian genie bottles, mushroom lamps and original Kartell Componibili side tables flows through the rooms. Dann has been a collector of 1960s and 1970s design for twenty years, drawn to the colours and patterns of the decades and partly influenced by her best friend, Lisa, who also lives in a very cool throwback home.

Hunting and collecting helped Dann years ago when she was dealing with anxiety issues and wasn't able to drive around Sydney without experiencing panic attacks. As a sort of graduated exposure therapy, she would get in the car and take the short drive to the nearest thrift shop, where the thrill of uncovering an amazing piece would distract anxious thoughts and act like a reward. Soon enough, her drives were getting longer and she was visiting thrift shops, markets and antique stores all over; at the same time, her need to hunt down unique, original items grew stronger.

The whole family loves their spacious home, but Dann especially appreciates the room it gives her to display her retro collections.

Dann creates colour stories for each room. When the teak table set was added to the dining room, the colour theme went from teal to orange. The master bedroom also features orange tones (opposite).

The earthy side of the retro look is brought out with timber decor, such as the Danish candle holders above, as well as woven placemats and textured pottery. A Vladimir Tretchikoff print is the focus in a group of plant stands by the entryway (opposite).

She focused her attention on researching the pieces she was finding and soon discovered a network of like-minded retro-holics. She built up the confidence, and enough stock, to open Retrospectrum, a popular retro store that she successfully ran for three years.

When it came time for Dann, husband Arron and their girls, Molly and Lola, to escape the increasing hustle of Sydney, they shut up the shop and looked for a home in a serene coastal town south of the city. Scrolling through rental listings, Dann's sharply tuned eye zoomed in on this home's generous layout, the lofty angled ceilings and the copper-hooded fireplace surrounded by stone, all straight out of a 1976 issue of *Home Beautiful* magazine. The family had been living in a cluttered part of Sydney's inner city, and the idea of spreading out in a large, open space was appealing to everyone—there would be room to breathe. Molly and Lola love having their own bedrooms and the fact that they have views of trees out the windows. They love jumping on the trampoline, as Seamus explores the property and their dad sits in the backyard, strumming his guitar.

Dann isn't the only collector in the house: Arron works as a software architect but has had a lifelong obsession with music, playing in many bands and watching countless gigs. Their large home allows for an area dedicated to Arron's impressive collection of alphabetised albums and rows of bass guitars, as well as the space for jam sessions with his band mates. Arron enjoys the camaraderie of being in a band, but he also loves how, when playing his bass, he can completely zone out all distractions.

When Arron plays, everything else drops away from his mind, and he experiences only that moment. This meditative state is called 'flow', and it's exactly what Dann feels when she is rearranging things in her home. She is a natural at creating vignettes, skilfully bringing together clusters of objects and demonstrating textbook examples of the elements and principles of design. She gets completely absorbed in her puttering, persisting until that sense of satisfaction and calm washes over her once everything is sitting right.

Dann has reopened Retrospectrum in their south-coast neighbourhood, and the beautifully merchandised store continues to be a therapeutic outlet for her; it's another platform where Dann can focus her attention, get lost in puttering and share her love of retro with others. Molly and Lola think their home is pretty awesome—they especially love the angled ceilings and how close the beach is—but Dann and Arron know that the girls' own sense of style needs to be cultivated and not forced. There's a high chance that Molly and Lola will turn away from retro style and, just like the teenagers of the 1960s, they will assert their individuality and rebel against the way their parents live.

A mushroom lamp, vintage material framed by Dann and macramé hangings are at home next to the fireplace, the hero of this throwback living room.

To take one step into the
home is to understand that
a serious collector lives here.

Dann is fond of Donald Clark wall-hangings, as seen below and opposite in the bedroom. She has researched the Australian textile designer extensively and owns more than twenty unique pieces.

The secrets to vignette styling

Do you own special items collected over the years that you can't part with? They might be travel mementos, knick-knacks that you couldn't leave behind in a junk shop or meaningful objects passed down through your family. The way you display these treasured objects proudly in your spaces reveals a lot about who you are as a person. Grouped clusters—featuring sculptures, lamps, artworks, vases, ephemera, books and so on—add a layer of texture and story to a home. The trouble is, without some consideration, the well-intended displays can end up looking like clutter.

In other parts of this book, I have written about the categories of objects we collect, but this section covers the nitty gritty of creating vignettes with your collected objects. By observing the number of vignette-styling workshops that have popped up recently, and the volume of articles about the subject to which I have been asked to contribute, it would be safe to say that the still-life arrangement is something a lot of people are keen to master.

The key to creating a visually pleasing vignette lies in the convergence of art and science. Theories about visual perception explain how our brain reads groupings of objects (google 'Gestalt Theory of Visual Perception' to learn more), while 'elements and principles of design' cover the rules of composition. These theories and principles inform the basic visual guidelines I follow when I create a display (see opposite), but I prefer to frame the activity in a less-than-scientific way.

Imagine the vignette is a group of friends, hanging out. Think about it. It's a posse of pieces cruising along the mantle. It's a team of tchotchkes taking over the sideboard. A squad of stuff chilling on the coffee table. You get the idea. Consider the dynamics of a group of good friends. Each person brings their own quirks and backstory to the group, but commonalities among the friends keep them all together. There is harmony in the circle when everyone gets to be their own person while still fostering support for each other. They orbit in close proximity but never crowd one another. A group filled with friends who are way too similar has the potential to be monotonous, lacking the spontaneity that comes with a diverse bunch of people—sometimes a little tension keeps things interesting!

At the centre of my 'group of friends' framework is a focus on the relationships between the individuals (in other words, how they interact with each another). When creating a vignette, you need to scope out the arrangement in the context of how the group is working as a whole but also how the individual elements add their own dynamic to the group. Flip through this book and study all of the vignettes captured on the pages—I guarantee the groups of friends will reveal themselves to you. I hope this friendship approach helps you with vignette styling from here on in—it definitely adds an interesting edge to the activity!

The way you display your treasured objects in your home reveals a lot about who you are as a person.

Five basic guidelines for curating curios

1 Choose a surface or corner of the room that needs added texture and visual interest, but be practical about the positioning and go with a spot that can remain undisturbed. There is no point in setting up something that needs to be moved daily! The scale of the items you want to display determines the amount of space you need, and it's best to highlight the arrangement by allowing for some clutter-free space around it.

2 A vignette that contains too many objects runs the risk of looking cluttered, but there is no definitive answer to the question of how many objects is too many. However, if the group has fewer than three objects, there won't be enough visual tension in the arrangement. The relationships formed between colours, materials and sizes are more dynamic and eye-catching when you have three or more objects. In the context of my 'group of friends' framework, things get interesting when there's a third person to bounce off!

3 A thread of consistency in colour or material running through the objects will ensure that the individual elements relate to each other, even if they contrast in other ways. If there is nothing that ties the objects together visually, the collection will look bitsy and incoherent. I don't believe in rules about the number of colours or materials you should include in an arrangement—go with your gut, and then take a step back to see what gels for you and the space around the vignette.

4 Display objects that feature a variety of shapes and sizes, as repetition of the same shape or size can look monotonous and predictable. For instance, break up straight lines with curvy lines, or place short items next to tall ones. You don't want extreme differences, though, as disparate items will appear out of sync with each other. You do need a leader in the group, so pick a dominant object to be your focal point and relate everything else back to it.

5 Composition is king. Place your largest items first to build up the basic formation of your display, and then follow through with the smaller elements. If the items form a triangle shape, stepping down levels from the highest point, your eye will be led around the arrangement and it will read as more interesting. A symmetrical display—where one half is a mirror image of the other—looks formal, while an asymmetrical display (with its highest point off-centre) looks loose and casual. Don't forget about negative space within the arrangement—spots that are object-free can help make the individual elements easier to see and the total arrangement better to look at.

A bright,
welcoming
tribute to art
and heart

Sandra

A paddle and a portrait painted by Sandra Eterovic buddy up with a painting of two ladies by British artist Lizzy Stewart. The previous page features another of Sandra's works.

BUS STOP

Sandra

Sandra was funny. The illustrator and maker wasn't the kind of funny that placed her centrestage at social gatherings; she wouldn't have wanted to hog the spotlight like that. Her style of humour—subtle and wry—came out in her art practice and the things she gathered around herself in her home. I met her only once, over the weekend that we photographed her in her home for this book, but her easy manner and generous hospitality had us instantly chatting like old friends. It seems she had that effect on everyone; Sandra was well known in the Australian art community and had fans all over the world. Sadly, almost exactly one year after we spent time with Sandra, we received the devastating news of her passing.

Sandra shared twenty years of history with her home. The compact two-bedroom house was built in the early 1900s but had been stripped of period features over time. When Sandra purchased the property in her early twenties, it was a dark, narrow terrace that sorely needed heating installed to combat the chilly Melbourne winters. Once the heating was sorted, Sandra's stonemason father helped update the kitchen and bathroom with granite and marble countertops. Carpets were ripped up, floorboards were polished and skylights were installed to bring light into the rooms. The skylights did their job in the middle of the day, but as soon as the sun moved over during the afternoon, the home fell back into what Sandra called 'Victorian darkness'. Despite any glum lighting, this home was always bright with personality due to the colour and humour of Sandra's collections and her welcoming ways.

Sandra painted onto plywood and objects, and she was a dab hand at knitting, sewing and quilting. There was a folk-craft feeling to her aesthetic, but the flash of her dry, sharp humour stopped it from becoming too twee. Her colourful art reflected observations of modern life, and everyday characters were often given a surreal twist, such as the ladies with sausage legs, or the person wearing a cluster of cottages like a hat. A set of Russian nesting dolls she crafted included a teen in a tiger onesie plus a grizzly, dishevelled man—the largest doll of the pack—wearing a Chanel T-shirt.

Sandra stands in her narrow hallway, which could quickly turn into an obstacle course if she parked her bike inside. Her home was filled to the brim with her creations, as seen overleaf.

A bathroom cabinet filled with quirky packaging hangs on the wall beside a bird etching
by Bridget Farmer (above); a soft sculpture in a human form by French artist Nathalie Lété
looks towards an eclectic mood wall (opposite).

The characters Sandra painted were often based on people she had observed around Melbourne, a rich source of inspiration for this artist who loved to celebrate humans and all their flaws.

Inspiration also came to Sandra in the form of vintage packaging, children's books from decades past and the folk traditions of faraway places. Part of her childhood was spent on the Croatian island of Brac, where her parents grew up. Sandra soaked up every little detail of the Eastern European way of life in the early 1980s, from the colour palette of embroidered chair covers to the patterns on her cousin's exercise books and the decorative foil wrapped around a salami stick. Observe the Croatian national costume, with its intricate embroidery and lacework, and you get a sense of the kinds of patterns Sandra had stored in her memory bank. It is no surprise that the shade of bright red featured in the costume also happened to be Sandra's favourite colour and a hue that was repeated throughout her spaces.

Sandra's home was textured with a village's worth of unusual characters. Illustrated faces peered out from picture frames, while little flat plywood humans and anthropomorphic cushions monitored the daily happenings from their positions. Some of the furniture looked as if it could jolt into action and teeter right across the room at any moment. Sandra's brother built the unique plywood dining table for her after she sent him an image of a Moroccan table found in the pages of *The World of Interiors* magazine. The tongue-in-cheek design, delivered to Sandra as a flat pack, was usually topped off with a bright tablecloth and always surrounded by a quartet of timber dining chairs, one of which was painted in her favourite jaunty red.

Sandra was always a busy creative. Commissions steadily rolled in from publishers and retailers, and there was usually a gallery exhibition or two that she was working towards. She spent a lot of her time in her studio a few suburbs away, but cooking at home for friends and rearranging her collections were also favourite pastimes. Sandra would often tweak her two mood walls, one in the front room and the other near the kitchen, adding her latest inspirational finds and things that made her smile. She would arrange two- and three-dimensional elements—such as old masks, aged medical diagrams and small ceramic objects—mashing together a mix of concepts to create something new. This assemblage approach to wall decoration gave Sandra's small space an added layer of texture and youthful energy; the arrangements changed, but you could be sure they would always include quirky folk and cheeky characters.

Those closest to Sandra say that her life can be defined by 'her art and her big heart', and we will always have her village of faces to remind us of her warm, funny ways.

Fun pops of colour and Sandra's cheeky artworks invigorate plain walls. She designed these pillowcases for Australian fashion label Gorman.

Framed lithographs from the 1930s depict a range of Slavic costumes. Four unique chairs look quite at home around the plywood dining table (opposite).

136

How to add more texture to your home

If you come across a velvet couch or a silk-covered pillow, do you automatically run your fingers over the surface and smile? Do you reach for a hug from a loved one or pull a fuzzy blanket around you when you're feeling down? The sense of touch and physical connection is strongly tied to our affective state, and the right tactile experience can give us a much-needed boost through hard times.

Soft textures in the home have the same effect as a big, restorative embrace from a loved one. When you need to flop down on a sofa, you want it to be worn in and squidgy, rather than hard and unforgiving. This is not to say that other sorts of textures aren't good in the home. Rough, patinated textures make us think of the way natural materials age when exposed to the elements, grounding us in nature. Smooth, satiny textures make us think of high design and cleanliness. Some people will gravitate to the rustic, while others will be drawn to the sleek.

The key to working with texture in your home is balance. A room filled with only one type of texture will overwhelm the space; a room overflowing with a cacophony of competing textures will have the same effect. Just the thought of a room from the 1970s covered in floor-to-ceiling shag makes me feel itchy and stifled, despite the fact that I am a big fan of the interior design from the era. On the flip side, too much gloss and high shine will feel cold, like the steely, clinical ambience of an operating theatre.

You need to give your senses a relief, in the form of contrasting and complementary textures. The beauty of an individual texture is highlighted when it is placed next to a different texture—think about how effective it is to put a glassy glazed vase on a rustic timber tabletop, or a chunky woollen throw over a leather armchair. Embracing this kind of textural interplay will result in a room that feels good to be in and offers a wealth of interesting visual moments.

Finding a balance between textures in your home is important for your wellbeing.

Ten ways to inject texture

1 Layer up cushions and throws on your sofa to add comfort. They will also distract from the sofa's fabric if you aren't fond of it.

2 Embrace the imperfections of second-hand furniture and handmade objects. Wonky is good, and the signs of age can be beautiful.

3 Create a mood wall. Don't stop at artwork—add in wall-hangings, ceramic pieces, masks, cool packaging, postcards and so on.

4 Throw a rug down to instantly add an inviting texture to a tile or hardwood floor.

5 Pick natural materials for your home decor instead of overprocessed, machine-made ones. Timber, linen and leather have a warmth and tactility that gets better with age.

6 Decorate with pieces found in nature. Display a dish of pretty feathers on your coffee table, or dot dried seed pods on your shelves.

7 Fill your shelves with books that you love, and let them overflow to other parts of the house—stack them on tables, in tall piles against the wall or along a staircase.

8 Choose plants and floral arrangements that feature leaves and petals with exaggerated shapes. Go for large-leaved plants and generous, tall posies of flowers to really make a statement.

9 If you are designing a new home or renovating an old one, look at alternative surfaces for your internal walls and floors, such as cork and brick floors or corrugated sheeting walls.

10 Add ethically sourced animal hides, such as sheepskins or Mongolian furs, to sofas, chairs or at the end of the bed.

Playful spaces in a warehouse-turned-cubbyhouse

Leah & Wally

Leah Hudson-Smith
covered the second-hand
armchair in Kvadrat fabric.
Texture is added to a wall
with a display of woven
pieces, including flax
bags from New Zealand
and a fan from northern
Ghana (opposite).

Leah
&
Wally

/

When Leah was a young girl growing up in Auckland, New Zealand, she would spend her days building cubbyhouses. Beyond just throwing a sheet over two armchairs, Leah would create serious structures that weaved through doorways and required the repositioning of furniture to maximise the fort's footprint and flow. While most of us were just rearranging things on our bookshelves or creating pop-star montages on our bedroom walls, Leah was reimagining entire spaces and, much to her engineering father's delight, revealing her early interest in architecture and spatial relationships.

Talk to Leah about the residence she currently shares with her partner, Wally, in the inner suburbs of Melbourne, and you can tell that the home they have created is the result of her thoughtful approach to space planning, charged with the couple's shared need to keep life light and fun. Leah and Wally—an interior architect and a musician/tour manager, respectively—are a social couple who like to laugh, entertain and travel. Their open-plan warehouse home gives them plenty of space to host friends and the flexibility to change the layout when they need to combat the extremes of the Melbourne seasons. Their charismatic pooch, Benson the 'Prince of the North', pads around the space, taking his role as the unofficial doorbell seriously, alerting the couple to incoming guests with his deep bark. Bikes roll in next to the dining table, and their outdoor space—with its turf, potted plants and bench seating—resembles the sort of outdoor bar you would see on the buzzy main street just around the corner. So much so, strangers often pop their head into the warehouse's laneway entrance looking for a pint.

Wally is a born and bred Melburnian, having grown up only a suburb away. Besides an overseas gallivant in his early twenties and international tours with his band, he has resided and worked within a tight inner-city radius, including the time he lived behind a gourmet grocery store that he owned and ran with a close friend. The sense of community and the connection that Wally feels to the area are both very strong, as illustrated by the fact that his band members live in the large warehouse next door.

Leah Hudson-Smith, Wally Maloney and their dog, Benson, gather around a dining table made by Leah; a weaving from Myanmar hangs on the wall.

A snippet of Wally's record collection is shown above; music plays an important part in his life, just as the process of designing and making is essential for Leah. She hand-dyed the linen on the dining table, and she crafted the circular wall-hanging out of Tasmanian oak (opposite).

The bedroom pod is an intimate space where the temperature can be easily controlled. Once the fireplace was installed (opposite), the warehouse felt like a home.

Wally composes music on this century-old piano, sitting on a chair that Leah made with American oak. Above the piano is a lithographic print from Oaxaca, Mexico.

When the guys rehearse, their tropical-inspired party music filters through the streets. It was through friends that Leah and Wally came to live in this sensational space.

The warehouse's previous tenant, a talented woodworker that the couple knows, had turned what was once a grubby mechanic's garage into something habitable. He had cleaned away years of oil and grime, lined the ceiling in ply, put up bathroom walls and created a neat kitchen with American oak benchtops and exposed copper pipes, a good match to the industrial feel of the brick walls and concrete floors. Their friend had undertaken a huge amount of the grunt work, but Leah knew that the space needed a few more things before it could be considered 'home'. The big, open room was missing the private zones that a standard home would offer, particularly areas in which to sleep and work.

Leah, having taken her cubbyhouse-building prowess and turned it into a successful design career, took the opportunity to design two separate pod structures—sophisticated, grown-up versions of a cubbyhouse. The bedroom structure is made of maple and shaped like a child's line drawing of a house, with a pitched roof and a window off to one side. The interior of the maple house is painted white and minimally decorated, providing the couple with a calm and neutral space in which to sleep. Most importantly, the maple house can be completely closed off from the larger space to contain heat, sorely needed in Melbourne's chilly winters. The other structure is a charcoal-painted bunker-like box and the perfect insular hideaway in which Wally can work without interruptions. Shelves installed on the outside of the bunker create a library zone in the negative space between the two structures. With the help of a stonemason friend (in exchange for a bottle of whisky), they installed a fireplace, completing the transformation from warehouse to home.

Their home is filled with one-off timber furniture pieces that Leah has made through her calculated trial and error approach to creating. Because she is untrained in carpentry, Leah works instinctively, responding to the grain of the piece of timber in front of her. The process satisfies her deep-seated need to experiment and play. Her work includes a striking timber screen, two-dimensional pieces for the wall and many of the tables in the space, each with the attention to detail and finish you would expect from an interior architect.

The rest of the home is furnished with Gumtree discoveries or finds from the side of the road, and the objects, textiles and art carefully dotted around the lofty space have been collected over the many travels that Leah and Wally have done. As much as they love kicking back at home, they highly value their travel adventures and the inspiration these journeys provide. By decorating their home with pieces collected on their trips, they are constantly reminded of the experiences that define them. More importantly, they are reminded to keep playing and learning.

Travel mementos and plants dot the space. Below is a brass crab that Leah bought in Japan; the petite kitchen (opposite) will always be home to a plant or two.

What to do if you don't have a green thumb

Are you a green thumb or a plant assassin? I have a confession: I am terrible at keeping indoor plants alive. So I leave all the plant care to my husband, Beau, the keeper of the green in our home. While I don't feel comfortable about dishing out advice on plant maintenance, it would be remiss of me not to include words about our green friends in a book about homes with character.

As living organisms, plants bring a vibrant energy into a home. They require water, nutrients and sunlight, and in return they add texture and movement to our spaces, they freshen the air and they make us feel better about ourselves. In looking after a plant, we are given a purpose and are forced to slow down; our patience is tested, but we soon become connected with nature.

Just as the blue of the ocean has a calming effect on most of us, shades of lush green speak to us about freshness and wholesomeness. Plants make a space feel comfortable. The presence of a healthy plant indicates a certain kind of stability; it signals a happy, nurturing environment.

A room without plants can feel flat and lifeless, whereas a room filled with plants of all sizes and shapes will feel dynamic and texturally interesting. Indoor plants can also make a space feel bigger. Consider a tall potted plant that stretches to the ceiling, a trailing variety in a hanging basket or a vine growing on a wall; in each of these cases, our eyes are drawn up and around the room, emphasising the vertical and horizontal lines in the space.

The effect a plant has on a space is pretty magical, and the pure authenticity of something growing out of the dirt is unrivalled. However, if you (like me) have trouble keeping indoor plants alive, there are many other options you can consider.

You can reap the benefits of greenery in your home, even if you are a proven plant assassin.

Alternatives to pot plants

Soaked greens
If you can't stick to a watering schedule but still want to cultivate greenery, choose plants that can adapt to growing in water, such as the spider plant, philodendron and mother-in-law's tongue. Pop them into a clear glass vase or jar, top up the water when you notice the level dropping, give them some sunlight and keep checking the roots for rot.

Temporary leaves
Fresh-cut foliage will give your home a hit of green and can last longer than cut flowers. Make a bold statement with large monstera leaves or a thick mass of eucalypt vegetation in a weighty vase, and freshen the water every few days.

Synthetic styles
As much as I hate to admit it, the popularity of faux plants is on the rise. The market is flooded with cheap, tacky fakes, so it pays to hunt down the higher-quality versions. Take note of the leaf colour, the vein detail, the stem and the way the plant sits in its 'soil', and please steer clear of any styles with plastic raindrops on the leaves! Would you believe that some of the homes in this book feature artificial greenery? I wonder how easy it is for you to spot …

Leaf motifs
If all else fails, you can bring a botanical element into your space with art, cushions and decor that feature leafy patterns. While a wall slathered in vine-printed wallpaper won't freshen the air for you, it will definitely give the illusion of an indoor jungle.

An art-filled retreat where the kettle is always on

Gab & Mick

The home is warmed up with lamplight and the frequently used fireplace (opposite). The vintage twin-dome red lamp on this page was an online marketplace find.

158

Gab
&
Mick

/

Gabrielle and Michael are good people. Gab is a jeweller who runs a retail space with a workshop out the back, and Mick works for the local council and practises his own art. They live in a rural town, on a 2-hectare block overlooking ancient apple gums and a hill that kangaroos have made part of their daily traverse. They are the kind of couple you want to have as neighbours. The kettle is always boiling for the next cuppa, and their friendly, calm demeanour puts you at ease. They live in a historic area known for its dairy farming and rolling pastures; however, Gab and Mick's home is anything but country-quaint.

When the couple first saw the 1990s-built, double-storey brick home, they looked beyond the 'faux ski lodge' fit-out and salmon-coloured walls, and instead focused on the cathedral ceiling in the large living space and the mass of land that surrounded the house. The double-storey shed on the property allowed for the storage of Mick's cherished collection of vintage Toyota Land Cruisers and an area for the couple to create large-scale sculptures and artworks. They moved in and, without doing any major structural work to the house, were able to stamp the space with their own style by painting the walls, changing out the bland fixtures and fittings, and skilfully arranging an impressive collection of art and mid-century furniture.

Red walls sit adjacent to black walls, and the rich timber of the furniture and ceiling architecture glows with warmth, especially in the evenings when the couple reads by lamplight, tends to the fire and snuggles with their dogs, Doug and Phang. Their yellow-topped dining table is soaked by the morning sun and is the spot where many cups of tea are sipped and from which trespassing sheep are observed through the window. The visual cues of warmth in this house, and the daily rituals that play out, elicit the feeling of a big, enveloping hug, reflecting the friendliness that comes so naturally to the couple.

Gab and Mick are happiest when they are making and creating. Gab is formally trained in sculpture and worked for years with large steel constructions, turning to wearable art when she no longer had the space to create on a grand scale.

Gab McGrath and Mick Jarochowicz have made the house their own with simple cosmetic changes as well as a considered arrangement of their loved items.

Objects are arranged through the artist's trained eye, with an understanding of balance, colour and negative space.

A monochromatic artwork by Mick hangs above the staircase void. *Protozoan*, a copper and steel sculpture made by Gab, sits on a console and anchors an ever-evolving salon hang (opposite).

Off to Wonderland

Gab and Phang spend
a moment together in
the living room's dappled
afternoon light. Gab can
often be found reading on
the sofa in the bedroom
(above right).

Gab is drawn to yellow, red and the organic nature of round shapes. The latter often appears in her jewellery designs, as seen in her hands below.

The mid-century hutch houses sculptures by the couple, an ageing teddy bear that was rescued by Gab at a garage sale, and a porcupine made by their friend's three-year-old daughter.

Gab's work is inspired by a union of nature and architecture, and is always informed by environmentally sustainable practices. Mick, who studied visual arts and works across a wide range of media, also follows this approach to creation. Now that they have the space to work in larger formats again, the couple is creating together and has recently completed a scrap-metal sculpture for their property that they've positioned by the dam, within view of the house.

The couple's dedication to salvage and upcycling crosses over into how they go about making a home, favouring quality second-hand pieces over buying new. With a soft spot for original mid-century design, Gab has an uncanny ability to scoop up incredible finds at junk shops and auctions for next to nothing. The perfect pieces seem to fall into her lap, but the truth is that Gab is on a continual hunt for clean-lined timber furniture and interesting decor. She is a focused second-hand shopper, which shows in the careful edit of pieces in their space. They have filled their home with items they love, arranging them through the frame of their art training and with an understanding of balance, the power of colour and the value of negative space.

The art throughout the home has been collected by Gab and Mick over the years and includes many pieces that the couple has made. Gab's ever-evolving gallery wall is a mood-read of her latest art obsessions, sourced through social media or local art shows. The town in which they live boasts a large regional gallery and a thriving artistic community; through her retail space located on the main street, Gab has been introduced to many local artists who have become good friends.

When Gab and Mick get home, Doug and Phang—eager for walks, treats and pats—greet them at the front door. They catch up with their neighbours over the boundary fence, swapping stories about snake or fox sightings and sharing vegies. The water is put on the boil, and the couple settles in for a quiet night most evenings. Although they are a friendly, welcoming pair, the favourite thing these homebodies like to do is to bunker down in the warm space they have created, just the two of them and their doggie duo.

Mick keeps the scrap-metal pile meticulously categorised. The wax sculpture (opposite) was made by Mick of his previous dog—and cherised old mate—Ceda. The red cattle dog was born deaf, so the pair communicated with gestures developed over their 14 years of being together.

Hairy housemates: living with pets

——

For those of us who have pets, there is no doubt that these creatures play an important part in our home life. Does your daily routine bend to these furry family members? Do your house rules accommodate their comings and goings? Seats in the house are often reserved for pets, and our fur children can influence our sleeping schedule. Pet hair is a constant, and paw prints show up in places you least expect. However, if we put up with these minor inconveniences, pets will fill the house with love and laughter, adding to the story and heartbeat of our homes.

It hurts my heart to see animal shelters filled with the surrendered pets that didn't meet the unreasonable expectations of their owners. Pets who excessively dig and chew or are A-grade escape artists are often acting out because they are anxious or bored. A consistently secure and nurturing home environment will foster a happy and obedient pet. Our furry friends need owners who are calm, patient and reasonable, and they need a life filled with regular walks and balanced diets.

Pets will fill the house with love and laughter, adding to the story and heartbeat of our homes.

Three tips for living with pets

1 Set boundaries, and be consistent. Pets don't know the rules when they first pad into your home. You need to invest the time to train them so that they understand when they are in the wrong, according to the rules that you set. You may run a household that doesn't believe in dogs on the sofa, or you may think that letting your dog into your bed is acceptable. However you see your pet fitting into your home, you must communicate the rules clearly to them. If, despite your best efforts, your pet just won't abide by the rules, then call in a professional trainer.

2 Learn to compromise, and don't be precious. No matter how well trained your pet is, there are certain things you can't control: fur will shed, and clouds of stink will fill the air. Frequent bathing and grooming sessions for your pet will help keep this kind of mess to a minimum, and it's handy to have furniture with slipcovers that can be washed, or machine-washable blankets. Our scruffy dog, Charles Barkley, knows that the blanket-covered section of the sofa is his spot to sit, and we give him a good brush twice a week. We still chase puffs of fur around the house, but it's a small price to pay for seeing his funny little face every day.

3 Observe and play daily. My favourite part of the day is coming home to Charles Barkley and having a waggy-tailed tussle with him. He goes through phases when it comes to the toys he likes, so we keep the current favourites accessible and neatly corralled in a shallow basket on the floor, while the neglected lot get stored in a cupboard and then reintroduced over time. Keep in tune with what is entertaining your pet, as there is no point in cluttering up your house with pet toys and accessories that get ignored.

A country homestead filled with family

Georgie, Matt, Donny & Ada

Butterflies—symbolic of joy and new life—feature heavily in the artworks that Georgie Stuart creates and displays around the home.

Georgie, Matt, Donny & Ada

Georgie, Matt and their sweet little ones, Donny and Ada, live in Bimlow Cottage, in a tiny village three hours' drive west of Sydney. Their community is made up of as many homes as you can count on your fingers and toes, spread out over the main road and a ring road. A deer farm surrounds the original schoolhouse, and the peaked roof of the old dance hall—now an artist's home and studio—sits behind a picket fence and protective trees. The area is known for its lakes filled with trout and as the spot keen fisherman and holidaymakers would park their caravans and trailers. Supplies were available to buy from the front room of Bimlow Cottage, the cute 1890s building that sat beside the caravans.

Georgie saw the listing for the cottage when she and Matt were living in a busy Sydney suburb, before the arrival of Donny and Ada. Her heart went out to the weatherboard home, with its rusty tin roof, chimneystack and garden stippled with daffodils; the caravans were long gone. Georgie had a gut feeling that this was the house in which the couple would raise a family. Papers were signed, and Georgie and Matt were soon spending their weekends at the cottage, painting, taming the rambling gardens and pulling out old picnic tables and swing sets, remnants from the caravan-park days.

They spent a year with one foot in the country and one foot in the city, and then decided that they had had enough of the urban hustle; they made a permanent move to Bimlow Cottage, not knowing at the time that they had already begun their family. Two quickly became three with the arrival of Donny, and three years later they welcomed Ada to the world.

At Bimlow Cottage, Donny chases chickens and sheep around their paddock while Matt tends to the grounds. Georgie loves to cook in the cosy kitchen, and Ada helps by pulling fresh ingredients from the vegie patch. The house and its quiet location have gifted the family with lots of quality time together. Matt takes Donny out on camping trips, visiting the local fishing and dirt-bike riding haunts, and the whole family loves to amble through the landscape, collecting feathers, discarded bird's nests and butterfly wings as they go.

The family comes together in Bimlow Cottage's cosy kitchen, sitting at the long, narrow dining table on the matching bench seats.

The artwork above the bed was embroidered by Georgie onto vintage linen; its delicate
nature is reflected in two paintings by Susie Dureau (above). The family loves to spend time on
the verandah (opposite), but they retreat indoors to the warmth of the fire in the harsh winter.

A salon hang by the fire includes works by Georgie, a print by an art-school friend plus thrift-shop pieces. The spare bedroom (opposite) features an old sign that came from Georgie's grandmother's antique store.

When Georgie and Matt's closest friends drive in from the city, they will usually spread their stay out over one or two nights, making it a proper catch-up at a slower pace. Meals are lingered over, sunrise cups of tea are shared on the verandah's pink-velvet lounge, and time is always made for a walk around the village to meet the young family's new friends. Even though Matt is busy with full-time work as a design manager in an engineering firm and Georgie juggles part-time work as a university project officer, the couple feels that their home in the country has given them the gear shift they were looking for, providing the perfect place to raise a family.

Ask Georgie about what makes Bimlow Cottage her home, and she will say it's the people in it and the moments she shares with those people. That isn't to say she doesn't love the 'stuff' of the house—the furniture, the collections, the everyday doodads—mostly vintage and gathered up by Georgie over the years. Georgie is drawn to old things, loving the patina of time past and the nostalgic beauty of chipped and scratched surfaces. She was exposed to the charm of the old world from an early age—her mum is a collector, and her grandmother has been running an antique store for forty years, a large emporium that Georgie tries to visit as often as she can.

The antique aesthetic follows through in the art that Georgie produces. She trained in fine art once she finished high school, and after a tragedy in the family, she was mysteriously driven to create work featuring beautiful butterflies. She embroiders richly coloured butterflies onto fabric and paints them onto textured surfaces such as scraps of rusted tin. Georgie's artwork is at home among her collections of delicate children's dresses, timber hatstands and handsome old hardcover books. Donny and Ada are her two very willing butterfly-hunting assistants, always on the lookout when they take their cherished family walks.

The family will be moving out of Bimlow Cottage soon, but they are only going as far as the paddock next to the cottage. Georgie, ever the vintage hunter, found a sweet old house for sale on Instagram and fell in love. The early 1900s-built home was in a town 200 kilometres away, so the couple had the building relocated and dropped onto their paddock, where the caravans once sat. Matt has painstakingly restored the house, opening up the ceilings, adding in big windows and extending the verandah, giving the family room to spread out and grow. The beautiful homestead is now one of the first buildings to greet you as you enter the quaint village, standing solid on the ground, symbolic of the young family's next stage of life in the country.

The slouchy, second-hand sofa and the global textiles, as well as Georgie's unique artworks of seaweed specimens drawn onto stitched teabags, create a rich texture in the corner of this room.

They feel that
Bimlow Cottage
is their home
because of the
people in it and
the moments
they share.

Family time is valued in the cottage, but if Georgie needs to slip away to focus on her art, the sunroom doubles as her studio, where she displays inspirations and stores her materials (detail at left).

Your stuff and how to live better with it

———

What kinds of things do you own? Do they make you happy, or do they cause stress? It has been said that the objects we curate around ourselves tell the story of who we are, where we've been and where we are dreaming of going next. Our stuff is an outward expression of our inner selves, of what we are and are not. The atmosphere of a home is made up of a combination of many things—reinforcing people's stories in ways that appeal to all the senses—but it is the layer of objects in a home that is the most tangible expression of self.

I like to categorise home stuff in three different ways: *functional* stuff helps us carry out the minutiae of our days (toasters, toothbrushes, plates); *decorative* stuff adds polish to our spaces (vases, cushions, art); and *sentimental* stuff comprises the pieces that have been handed down through generations, or things that are directly tied to important moments in our lives.

The key to living harmoniously with your stuff is to find a balance between these categories in your home. If everything you own is purely functional, with nothing that appeals to the emotions, your space will feel like a mechanic's workshop, filled to the brim with lifeless equipment. If your stuff is purely decorative and perfectly placed, your home will feel like a museum of style or a showroom setting behind glass. A house filled with family heirlooms sounds like a heartwarming idea, but it has the potential to feel stifling and psychologically heavy with inherited stories of the past.

The goal is to surround ourselves with items that tick the box for all three categories. A beautiful working clock passed down through family members is not only emotionally rich but also functional, and it can be enjoyed on a daily basis. When you pour breakfast cereal into a handmade bowl you picked up on a holiday, good feelings associated with the trip resurface and you start your day on a positive note. These psychological reactions may only be slight—if you are conscious of them at all—but over the span of a day, week, month or year, they combine to reinforce the story of you.

It is the layer of objects in a home that is
the most tangible expression of self.

Collection vs clutter

A collection:
🌢 is an accumulation of objects, chosen carefully and often over time;
🌢 can be a serious investment, such as art or cars, or a simple pleasure, such as pretty feathers found on walks;
🌢 is displayed intentionally and with care;
🌢 gives people joy and enhances the time they spend in the home; and
🌢 reminds people about who they are.

Clutter:
🌢 is an accumulation of daily debris and forgotten things;
🌢 often has no emotional or financial value;
🌢 is stuffed into drawers, cupboards and boxes;
🌢 can cause feelings of guilt, shame and anxiety; and
🌢 reminds people of the chores that need to be done.

A high-voltage
creative world
by the sea

Adam & Nick

Ken Done's print titled
*Ultramarine and Jade
Coral Head* and a neon
'Love' light set the mood
for the living room. Internal
windows peak into the
bright sunroom where
Adam Powell and Nick
Bond sleep.

Adam

&

Nick

/

This is a home that changes as often as the mood of the ocean. Wall colours and layouts never rest, and adjustments effortlessly roll through at the skilled hand of Adam, a stylist and installation artist with an appetite for high-voltage colour. He has lived in this seaside location for eight years, while his partner, Nick, moved in two years ago.

The compact east-facing apartment sits behind a semi-detached home built in the 1940s; light is scarce at the back of Adam and Nick's one-bedroom flat, but the sunshine starts to filter through as you step towards the windows of the sunroom and into the backyard. The couple spends a lot of time in these two spaces, drawn to the outdoors and the glimpse of the ocean at the end of their street. Not long after moving in, Adam relocated the bedroom from the cave-like room at the back of the apartment to the window-lined sunroom, so that Saturday mornings could be spent drinking coffee in bed while soaking up the sun and peeking into the greenery of the garden with the deep blue sea beyond.

The backyard, cultivated by Adam, is the most outdoor space Nick has lived with since he moved out of home when he was twenty years of age. He grew up in Melbourne, in a suburb at the foothills of the Dandenong Ranges, and spent weekends hiking and camping with his father. He built up a career in journalism in Sydney, spent a year in London and then returned to Australia, hungry for the sun and sparkling landscapes.

Adam's formative years on the north coast of New South Wales instilled in him a fascination with all things marine-related, from the majestic creatures that glide through the depths, to the energy of the waves, the electric colour palettes of tropical fish and the texture of rocky cliff faces that break the inky limits. Adam loves to surround himself with flashes of neon, a throwback to growing up in the 1980s, but his home also sings with raw, natural textures; this combination of colour and texture is characteristic of his refreshing aesthetic. Hold up a vintage fishing float—made up of timber and neon paint—and you have the essence of Adam's style in your hand.

Adam and Nick spend a lot of time in their backyard, surrounded by leafy greens and other natural tones.

A high-voltage creative world

The home is covered
in evidence of Adam's
creativity, from works in
progress and objects he
has crafted to beautiful
traces of his previous
professional projects.

A corner of the bedroom
works well as a desk nook,
with a painting by Adam
standing by. Nick's favourite
cushion (above) is inspired
by iconic Australian movie
Muriel's Wedding.

Adam's ideas have no limits—his inspirations crisscross the world—but he always finds a way to manifest his surreal dreamscape visions, with a focus and drive that attracts some of Australia's most well known brands. The cascading canopy of blue and green ribbon that sits above Adam and Nick's bed is a small section of an installation that Adam was commissioned to create for a seasonal launch at the Sydney Theatre Company. Adam and his good friend, Tamara, sat in his home and hand-tied nearly 90,000 ribbon lengths to create a canopy that ran for 50 metres. By the time the duo had finished assembling the colossal piece, their fingers were raw and the tiny flat was covered in a rustling sea of ribbon waves.

The compact home doubles as Adam's art studio, and the entire space, inside and out, is often covered in drop cloths to collect the detritus of making. The natural light of the backyard and sunroom is most conducive to fiddly craft work, so Adam finds himself assembling, gluing and painting in these areas the most, even if that means the mattress has to be dragged into the living room for the couple to sleep at night.

The home is a testing ground for Adam's creative work, always admired by Nick and allowed by a trusting landlord. The couple jokes that their home, charming in its dinky nature and old age, is held together by the wallpaper and paint that Adam regularly applies to the walls. Nick loves watching the ideas come together in their space, appreciating how the deft work of the clever stylist transforms the feeling of their home. Not long after the images were photographed for this chapter, the jungle wallpaper behind the bed was replaced with teal-coloured panels, and the black wallpaper in the living room had been swapped out for a faux-stone wall finish, completely changing the mood of the house and giving it a carefree, Palm Springs vibe.

Air sprayed with sea salt washes through Adam and Nick's home, and the couple jumps into the surf at Australia's most iconic beach located at the end of their street whenever they can, often followed by twilight drinks in their backyard. Their apartment is small but energised by the morning sunshine and Adam's never-ending quest to curate a colourful world around him, which is a mission that Nick fully supports.

The couple jokes that their home is held together by the wallpaper and paint that Adam regularly applies to the walls.

Adam's props are stored on shelves that his brother built, positioned near the dark
back room (above). Colourful timber pieces that he created for an installation lean
against a wallpapered wall (opposite).

The installation-artist approach to homemaking

Are you keen to bring artistic expression into your home, but you don't know where to start? Talk of art in the home usually revolves around the style, size and colour palette of a piece for the wall. Framed or unframed? Abstract or figurative? Calming blues or stimulating reds? Displaying wall art is an effective way to add energy and depth to a space, but I feel there are bigger home-decorating lessons to learn in other areas of the art world. To discover what will alter the look and mood of a room, simply observe the way an installation artist influences their immediate surroundings.

An installation artist transforms the perception of a space and curates an atmosphere by positioning objects and manipulating light, sound and smell. They reimagine objects, repurpose materials and play with scale to help make personal or political statements. Working outside the confines of a wall-mounted frame, the artist offers their audience the opportunity to physically interact with their ideas; they appeal to all of the senses, challenge expectations and impart a narrative. The artist wholly owns the space for that temporary moment, and their state of mind is reflected at that very specific point. They are completely exposed, but the motivation to share seems to override any inhibiting insecurities. Art and life merge as viewers walk through the artistic expression, gaining insight into the ideas and impulses of the artist.

When we adjust the atmosphere of our own spaces and position our objects just so, we are satisfying our need to establish a sense of ownership and to spread our own viewpoint. Even a small-scale gesture, such as deciding to store your tea towels in an old timber fruit box or switching on your favourite tunes, is an expression of your desire to curate your immediate world. The beauty of experimenting in our homes, our private spaces, is that we don't have to share our creations with anyone. There is no beard-stroking art critic ready to tear the work apart, or finicky public keen to write us off. If our experimenting doesn't go to plan, or if we get bored with one of our ideas, guess what—we can alter it!

In the same way that an ephemeral installation mirrors an artist's point of view at a particular time, our homes should echo our changing mind states and life stages. The billowing satisfaction and pride felt when we create and curate something for our homes is a feeling that's hard to beat.

Installation art can teach us how to curate our homes and express our personal narratives.

Think like an installation artist and use …

Repetition
Displaying things en masse creates a strong focal point and makes a clear statement about what you value. Pick a wall on which to hang a group of similar objects, or take over a shelf—or whole bookcase—with a collection of one category of thing.

Humour
A bit of irreverence in a room shows off the lighter side of life and adds a loose casualness to the air. It could be added through a cushion with a cheeky embroidered slogan or a risqué decor element. You may find humour in the juxtaposition of eras or origins, such as using a plaster bust as a hat holder, or displaying a contemporary photograph in an ornate gilt frame.

Sensory appeal
Consider how smell and sound influences your mood. If there is a particular scent that releases positive feelings in you—for example, the smell of burning sage or the fragrance of a tropical flower—then don't hold back when bringing that aroma into your space. The same applies to music— play the tunes that cut to the core of who you are, and be present with the sounds.

Salvage
A home that incorporates the clever re-use of discarded objects or the nifty repurposing of materials will be all the more unique and interesting. Salvage can be easily injected in smaller amounts (for example, using a vintage tea chest as a bedside table) or as big-picture thinking (such as incorporating exposed railway sleepers into the architecture of the building).

Scale
An oversized object will add a playful dynamic to a room and create drama. A larger-than-life lamp or a chair with wonky proportions will pull our attention and bring a room to life, challenging our expectations of what feels 'right' in a space.

Light
Bright light can make us feel uncomfortable and exposed, but it is necessary when we are doing a task that needs strong illumination. Subtle, moody lighting will make a space feel womb-like and cosy, but it isn't conducive to study or reading time. The trick is to establish a lighting scheme in your home that allows you to switch between different levels of illumination for a variety of activities. For more on lighting, see pages 252–3.

A graceful cottage filled with traces of the past

Helene & Quilla

Helene
&
Quilla

/

Helene, an archaeologist and visual artist, is drawn to the beauty of the everyday. In her archaeological work, she digs through built-up layers of earth to uncover fragments of human behaviour and piece together the stories of how people used to live. Her art explores thickly layered collages in subdued tones and photography that evokes both dreamy nostalgia and hazy melancholy. Her artworks adorn her home, as do objects and furniture pieces that wear the knocks of the past and tell the tales of times gone by. Helene is attracted to faded beauty, the sort of romantic notion of decay that you would find in a wilting rose or a cracked china teacup.

Helene's home is soaked through with a warm, worn tactility. Rich, dark, timber floors span the two-bedroom house, and a heaving cabinet of curiosities—a vitrine filled with archaeological artefacts, precious family heirlooms and found natural elements—sits in the living room, flanked by a mass of books. Helene's reference library feeds her inspiration daily, as do the flowers she ritualistically buys each week to dress the house. She lives with pieces that have been handed down her family line and has collected other pieces that take her back to special moments throughout her life. The lantern in her bedroom reminds her of one that her grandmother had in her house in Greece, where a young Helene would visit to connect with her extended family.

Helene lives in the home with her teenage daughter, Quilla, and the two spend every second weekend out in the country. But it is her 1928-built cottage, located in a quiet suburb a stone's throw from the busy Melbourne CBD, to which Helene has a strong emotional connection. At her first inspection of the home, with baby Quilla attached to her hip, Helene had a vision of where the Christmas tree would sit. Even though the house was dark and intense, with garish colours on the walls and a peculiar humming energy that she partially attributes to the fact that a Wiccan witch used to live there, Helene purchased the property and quickly set about making it her own. She renovated the back of the house, doubling the footprint of the tiny kitchen and opening it up to the outside with French doors. A keen gardener who finds the work therapeutic, Helene tamed the wild, fertile garden and its row of fruit trees.

Helene Athanasiadis and her daughter, Quilla Diaz, at their dining table. A photographic print by Helene titled *Storm Tree* makes a dreamy statement on the wall.

Haigha Bugsy Rabbit by Kyoko Imazu overlooks kitchen shelves that are stacked with vessels found in thrift shops or made by Victorian artisans.

Helene, on a constant hunt for inspiration, finds joy in shelves heaving with books. The cabinet houses artefacts that are meaningful on personal, cultural and historical levels.

Helene's archaeological work inspires her art practice, through the notions of layering, patina and decay, and the telling of lost and forgotten stories.

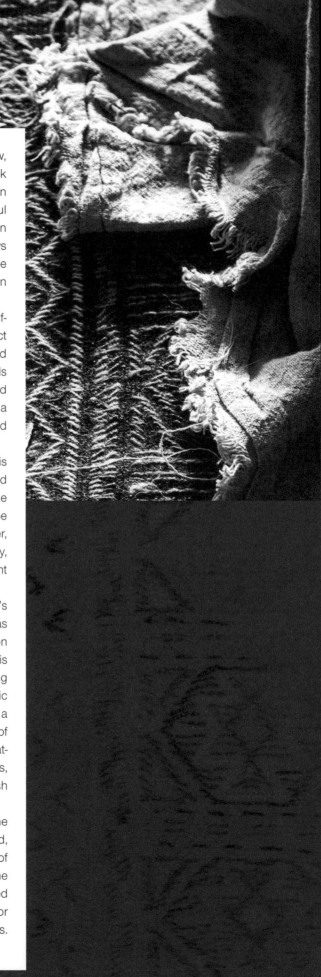

Afternoons are a lovely time to be in the kitchen, as the low, strong sun streams across the garden and through the back doors, classical music plays and pots of good food bubble on the stove. The calm of this space reflects Helene's graceful demeanour; she is a warm, natural host who finds great joy in the process of cooking. Helene has nurtured a home that allows her to recharge; it is a place in which she can find a balance between her physically and mentally demanding day job and an unyielding urge to create.

The idea of the private space and how important it is for self-preservation forms the basis of Helene's photographic project known as 'Solace', a documentation of women's solitude and the restorative places that provide respite from the daily demands of family, work and self-inflicted pressures. Her solace is delivered by spaces dedicated to preparing for the day, spaces that offer a meditation and links to the ancient rituals of cleansing and adorning armour for battle.

Helene's dressing room off her quietly decorated bedroom is such a space. The small room with a large window and textured grey walls is layered with rugs and filled with special vintage pieces—furs, hats, fragile dresses—and a skilfully edited wardrobe in a muted, elegant palette. Her training as a fashion designer, the career she established before she turned to archaeology, tuned her eye to the art of a well-crafted garment and a penchant for classic, iconic labels.

The bijou bathroom also plays an important part in Helene's ritual of preparation. When she first moved in, the wet room was dingy and depressing; it was covered in rusty corrugated iron and had an equally rusty bathtub. Helene loves patina, but this kind of corrosion didn't sit well with her need for a clean, soothing space. The original claw-foot tub was re-enamelled, and classic subway tiles replaced the corrugated iron. With the addition of a vintage medicine cabinet, a vanity that was found on the side of the road (the perfect size to squeeze into the tight space), a flat-weave mat for the floor and a rotation of freshly cut flowers, Helene has created a space where she can ceremoniously wash off the previous day and start afresh with the new.

Archaeological digs are physically demanding, but the romance of finding traces of the past keeps Helene energised, inspiring not only her creative pursuits but also the aesthetic of how she lives and the importance she places on the rituals of the everyday. Helene spends her working days in steel-capped boots and dusty khakis, but she will always have a soft spot for gorgeously delicate dresses and the feminine beauty of flowers. Especially roses.

The dressing room is one of Helene's long-term dreams realised. The small room is bathed in light from the windows that view the backyard.

The cherished antiquarian books were a gift from Helene's late brother; he bought them
from Portobello Road market in London. Her bedroom (opposite) is decorated with a collage
she created and objects that remind her of her Greek heritage.

Preparing for the day is like a meditation for Helene, with links to the ancient ritual of adorning armour for battle.

218

Velvety roses and a burning candle complement the unexpected romance of an etching by Australian artist Kevin Mortensen titled *You can't help who you fall in love with*.

Rituals and how they connect you to your space

Do you have any rituals in your home? During the week, I look forward to the lazy weekend breakfasts we cook in our happy, yellow kitchen. I'm on the pans, while Beau looks after the coffee. We play music and dance around the dog. We pop toast and sprinkle herbs from our garden over the meal, sitting at the kitchen table, taking our time with the food and enjoying the idea of the free day ahead. When the week gets too much for me, I take solace in knowing that our sunny weekend breakfast is coming up.

Our homes should make us feel both comfortable and safe. They should envelop us in positive feelings and offer a sense of calm and stability when the outside world is tough and unpredictable. Rituals within the home infuse the space with a sense of value and meaning, heightening our connectedness and sense of belonging to ourselves, to each other and to our personal spaces.

Rituals are repeated activities that mark moments, creating a familiar rhythm and adding a real sense of significance to our everyday life. They can be gestures as simple as lighting a candle when the sun sets, or events with a bigger scope, such as a monthly dinner party at home with close friends. Even the ritual of making the bed every morning—a mundane task that many people skip—can adjust your headspace and set you up for a productive day.

The ritual can be a solitary ceremony that recalibrates and grounds your sense of self, or it can be a shared moment that connects you with those you love. Rituals that include the whole family will foster a stable home environment and generate warm, positive memories.

At the core of any ritual is the idea of taking time out to be in the moment of the significant activity, leaving everything else behind and focusing on the singular event. The rituals we choose to create and maintain in our homes are a reflection of our values and our goals. Rituals that focus on social interactions say something about how we value relationships and the importance of belonging and feelings of connection. Solitary rituals highlight a drive to stay strong from within, with the idea of self-preservation as the motivating force.

By maintaining rituals in your home, no matter the scope or frequency, you connect yourself to your space. The location becomes an important part of the moment, and the good feeling associated with the ritual is transferred to all the bits and pieces that surround you. Your rituals add to the layers of who you are and strengthen the bonds with others, and it's wonderful to know that our homes can play an important part in that process.

Rituals within the home infuse the space
with a sense of value and meaning.

Recommended rituals

If you feel that your home life could benefit from more marked moments, use the following list as a starting point to find your own rituals.

🌢 Take the time to brew a tea or coffee, and use a mug that is pleasant to hold. Ignore all your screens, sit in your favourite chair and enjoy every sip.

🌢 You can't beat a Sunday roast for the delicious aroma it sends through the house, and a plate of home-cooked food simply makes you feel good. Elevate the weekly occasion by setting the table with candles and napery.

🌢 Blast your favourite music or play an interesting podcast as you do the household chores.

🌢 Spend Saturday morning in your garden or tending to your potted greenery. Get the kids involved, and you will all see the benefits of digging through soil and caring for plants.

🌢 Run yourself a bath once a week, using your favourite soaps and beauty balms, and luxuriate in the quiet.

🌢 Arrange a vase of flowers or foliage each week, and place it somewhere prominent. Enjoy the act of arranging flowers, and appreciate the arrangement each time you pass by it.

✳ 'How could I possibly find the time to arrange flowers or sit in a bath?' I hear you ask. The answer comes down to using your precious time wisely. Think of the hours that are spent on social media, and how the mindless content can leave you feeling anxious and empty. Cut back on screen time (delete apps from your phone if you have to), and you will find yourself with more time to spend on yourself and your loved ones.

A rich oasis
of curated
objects

/

Matthew

Matthew

/

To sit in Matthew's apartment is to explore the world and voyage through time. Although his home is filled with museum-quality pieces, Matthew's warm and inviting space is far removed from the austerity usually associated with dusty, silent halls of untouchable relics. Here, soft music tinkles, the supple leather sofa begs you to slouch into it and objects are rich with sentimentality; Matthew cherishes these items for the personal memories they contain.

This stylish oasis is situated above the hurried streets of Melbourne's CBD, in a 1911-built building that once made up part of the city's rag trade. That the building is tied to Melbourne's industrial past is fitting for a man who has a deep-seated appreciation of history, on both a global and personal level. Matthew's own story starts with his childhood in England; he then lived, worked and studied across the globe in vibrant places such as Madrid, Cyprus and New York. Time spent in his youth working for an antiques dealer piqued his interest in the provenance of objects and cemented an aesthetic that spans a wide range of cultures and centuries.

For a man who has lived in many parts of the world, home for Matthew is wherever he displays significant objects and stacks his many hats. In this apartment, a whale's rib bone lies in front of a Louis XVI–period commode, which sits beside a 1940s blue chair he found on the streets of New York at three in the morning. A 1980s circular marble table is topped with rustic timber bowls and flanked by Chippendale carved chairs from the 1700s. The L-shaped sofa is layered with textiles from Turkey, Laos, Morocco and Australia; above this arrangement sits a woven mask from Papua New Guinea and a painting from Western Australia, dated 1914.

He takes great joy in collecting and curating meaningful objects, layering up the rooms with textiles in his favourite 'tired colour palettes' and giving old pieces a new context. Ask Matthew about anything in his home, and you are presented with an encyclopaedia's worth of information, delivered in the most engaging and charming way.

The grey metropolis outside Matthew Lucas' apartment sits in stark contrast to the warm, layered space he has curated for himself.

Matthew's textile collection represents a rich variety of cultures, while drinking tea in
Coronation china connects him to his own heritage. The dining-table vignette (opposite)
includes a timber stool from Ethiopia, pears in an Aboriginal carrying vessel, and resin
pieces from iconic Australian brand Dinosaur Designs.

A mask from Papua New Guinea disguises a bland wall light; the framed, unsigned English painting from the 1800s was the first piece of art Matthew bought, at the age of fourteen.

He absorbs international interior and fashion magazines as readily as he does historical biographies and reference books, and his Instagram account tracks the many museums and galleries he visits every week. Currently working as a business development manager for luxury brands, Matthew is an aesthete who chases inspiration; when it comes to dressing his home, however, he trusts his instinct and goes with what he absolutely loves and holds dear. The teddy bear his father gave his mother during their courtship sits next to a clock that his grandfather once owned; it is these sorts of items that build a meaningful space for Matthew, tapping into a sentimentality that makes the apartment feel secure and nurturing.

As passionate as he is about pieces with heritage, Matthew has a surprisingly measured approach to collecting. If he sees something brilliant in an antique or second-hand store, but he has no space or use for it, he will reposition the object so that it has more of a chance of being purchased and taken to a loving home. Matthew is motivated by the thrill of a find and a need to share beauty with others, but he also keeps his consumption under control, strictly editing his collections so that each piece has the opportunity to breathe. Prior to living in Melbourne, Matthew was located in Western Australia, where he has left a lot of his possessions behind in storage, including a massive library and artworks that couldn't be accommodated on the walls of this one-bedroom Melbourne rental.

When Matthew first moved in to this rental, he enjoyed the double-height ceilings and the wall of glass overlooking the city, but he despised the dated fit-out—in particular, the kitchen with its garish orange cabinets. The building was constructed in the early 1900s, but the apartment conversion in the 1990s resulted in rooms filled with passé fittings and fixtures. Matthew has been able to cleverly downplay certain elements to turn the space into something he loves. With permission from the landlord, the orange kitchen cabinets were painted over with a sophisticated grey. The bland light sconces are hidden by masks, layered rugs on the floor distract from the dull carpet, and decorative objects—such as the tall Vatican City flag in the corner by the sofa—add height without having to bang more hooks into the walls.

Matthew knows this isn't his forever home—next on the list is a country house with a garden and room for a library—but the idea of living in a space that isn't comfortably layered with meaningful pieces seems alien to him. Things that represent the past will always be with him, and the stories of those things will always warm up his spaces.

A dramatic West African headdress on a plinth and a boomerang from the deserts of Western Australia frame Matthew's favourite section of the leather sofa.

Rare Indian dowry sacks
sit above boots worn by
players of Buzkashi, a type
of polo from Afghanistan.
Sentimental items and
natural elements are
displayed together on an
eighteenth-century chest
of drawers (opposite).

Matthew takes an edited approach to his collections, giving individual pieces a chance to breathe.

How to stamp your story on a rental

Are you a tenant who despairs of having a home that truly reflects your style and personality? When we rent a house, we are borrowing the space. These houses weren't built for us, and they weren't built for the people who will move in after us, but they temporarily become our own when we arrange our things in them, go through our daily routines and create memorable moments in them. The walls aren't always going to be the colour we want them to be, the floors may not give us the starting base we were hoping for and often the detail of the building structure looks tired (if any architectural detail exists at all).

Renting a home is a rite of passage, the first stop after careening from the family nest. It may be the first time we have had to share common rooms with people outside our circle of kin, and it's often the first time we have had to think about what furniture as well as bits and pieces go into rooms that aren't the bedroom. Budgets are usually restricted when we rent in our youth, as we are juggling study, entry-level jobs and the pull of a vibrant, glittery social life. Hung-over Saturdays are spent constructing flat-packed furniture and dragging home beat-up items found on the side of the road.

Current social trends in Australia's major cities have us renting well beyond the heady student years, as the cost of living keeps rising. We tend to hold back on setting ourselves up completely in a rental, waiting for that magical day when we can drop boxes of our things onto the floor of our perfect forever home, taking in the generous floor plan, the mass of natural light and the spot-on finishes. What we need to realise, though, is that unfortunately the perfect forever home can take a while to come around, and even then you are very lucky if you manage to nab a property that ticks all your boxes. Stamping your personality on the home and making it your own is important for your wellbeing and sense of connectedness, whether you are renting or you have moved into your not-quite-perfect forever home and renovations are a costly pipe dream.

Our homes should be infused with our stories,
even if the space is temporary and imperfect.

Ideas to help make a rental yours

Mix up the layout to work for you
Rooms are defined by the furniture that goes in them—a bed belongs in the bedroom, while a dining table fits in the dining room. The real estate agent may tell you that the room at the front of the house is a lounge room, but that doesn't mean you have to keep it that way. Take note of where you are drawn to at different times of the day and the conditions you need for certain activities. In Adam and Nick's home on pages 188–201, the bedroom was in a dark cave of a room, so the sun-loving couple converted the bright sunroom into their bedroom; the old bedroom then became a workroom and storage space. They love rising with the sun and starting their weekends with coffee and the papers in bed, soaking up the light.

Use rugs to downplay unattractive flooring
Laying down a rug is the quickest way to hide floors that are looking a little worse for wear or may be finished in a way you don't like. I am a believer in rugs laid on top of carpet—as long as the pile of each isn't too thick. Make sure you get the size right using the Goldilocks approach—a rug that is too small will look dinky, while a rug that is too big will suffocate the space. You need to find one that is just right.

Display art without hacking into the walls
Landlords aren't very fond of holes in the walls, which makes it hard for renters to display their loved art and framed works. Sticky hooks can be useful for hanging things that are lightweight, but they aren't so reliable for heavier pieces—and cheaper brands will pull paint off the walls, anyway. Large-scale art can look great casually leaning against a wall, whether it sits atop a sideboard or is placed on the ground. Shadow box frames can nestle onto shelves among your books and hold favourite items. For unframed prints on paper, washi tape and coloured painter's tape will temporarily affix the art to the wall. Work slowly and carefully when you need to remove the tape, though, so that the paint remains intact.

Change up the lighting
My least favourite thing when it comes to homes is cold, harsh fluorescent lighting. If you are stuck with a temperature of overhead lighting that you don't love, fill your rooms with lamplight for a cosy and comfortable ambience. If you don't mind the temperature of the light but aren't a fan of the fittings, get up close to see if you can swap out the shades without the need for complicated rewiring.

* The other option is to talk to your landlord. If you would like to paint or make other minor alterations, there is a good chance that they will give you permission to do so. Especially if you mention that the changes may add value to the property!

The warmth of timber and lamplight in a hidden-away hamlet

Jess & Beau

The laminate in the
kitchen is a shade
of yellow known as
'Harvest Gold', a
popular colour for
kitchens in the 1970s.

Jess
&
Beau

/

My husband, Beau, and I were crammed into a shoebox-sized studio in Sydney's rapidly gentrifying inner city and looking for an exit when we found our new home. We now live far from the urban hustle, in a small community of just eleven streets, surrounded by bush and waterscape in the world's second-oldest national park. Large numbers of holidaymakers visit our hidden-away hamlet during summer, but we get to enjoy the location all year round. Beau works as an audio engineer in the city, and my work as an interior stylist takes me all over, but our thoughts are never far from home. After years of high-volume living in Sydney, our home gives us the respite and fresh air for which we had been searching.

We bought the house from an elderly man named Brian, who had built the double-storey solid brick home for his family back in 1976 and had been living in it until he put the house on the market. We could tell that the process of listing the property was an emotional experience for him; he shuffled through the rooms, showing us the light switches (he had gotten pretty creative with the wiring, so we appreciated the explanations).

Brian also demonstrated the tools he would leave us, including an extendable clipper arm he fashioned to reach the avocados growing on the higher branches of the thirty-year-old tree in the front garden. He apologised for letting parts of the expansive garden go—he was in no shape to keep it tamed—but he pointed out the vegies, of which there were plenty. We asked if he was going to take the yellow dining chairs with him, and he kindly said that it didn't make sense to separate them from the yellow kitchen.

Our guests smile as they tell us that our house reminds them of their childhood, taking them back to their grandparents' home or a holiday house they stayed at in the 1970s or 1980s. Our neighbourhood has always been a popular holiday destination, especially from the 1970s when the only access road was finally sealed. For many people, the area is the source of sunny recollections of sparkling summer days, carefree times when tanning and smoking were thought to be harmless.

Beau Sherrard and I, along with our rescue dog, Charles Barkley, love to look out over the lush trees from the balcony.

A tea-towel print by Camilla Engman sits framed on the sideboard. The shelf vignette (opposite) features a framed greeting card plus an artwork on ply by Tammie Castles.

A small artwork I painted and a portrait from a thrift shop are displayed at the front entry; Beau plays his ukulele in spare moments. A wool rug in front of the built-in shelves (opposite) is the perfect spot for me to lie and read or to contend with Charles Barkley's determined affection.

The mid-century bedhead
with built-in side tables
came from an online
marketplace, and the
print above the bed
is by Sydney-based
Quercus & Co.

While some people shudder at the thought of living in a throwback house, it's that golden holiday feeling that strengthens our connection to our home and neighbourhood. The original kitchen and bathrooms were in immaculate condition, so we had no reason to tear them down. There were certain things we updated—the busy carpet had to go, fresh paint was a must and new light fittings instantly sharpened up the look of each room—but we love the feeling of living with one foot in the past, complemented by the meaningful bits and pieces we have collected over the years.

I am exposed to a dizzying amount of beautiful products and spaces through my work as an interior stylist. I can appreciate the beauty of an object or room regardless of the style or budget, but when it comes to our home, Beau and I are most comfortable living with vintage pieces, handmade items and things that are a little bit scuffed up. Our red-velvet sofa was a hand-me-down from my grandparents, and my dad found our sideboard at a thrift shop for a song.

Art fills the walls, and our books and records sit on the custom-built shelves that we designed and installed with Beau's dad. The shelves sit opposite a wall of cedar panelling; Brian's handiwork, it's a feature that we could never imagine painting over. Our evenings are illuminated by lamplight, which highlights the rich cedar wall and cocoons us in a hugging glow. If I close my eyes to think about the essence of our home, it's the warmth of timber and the happy hum of the yolk-yellow kitchen that shines through, a type of richness that has nothing to do with high-end design or glossy on-trend pieces.

There is always something to do at home. Beau tends to the garden most weekends, our scruffy rescue dog Charles Barkley needs walking often and, since we don't have a dishwasher—the downside of living with an original kitchen—there is usually a sink full of dishes to deal with. But when we take a moment to sit on our balcony overlooking the trees, that holiday feeling comes back. Sounds dance up from the water at the end of the street, with boats putt-putting and kids shrieking as they jump off the jetty.

A year after moving in, we started to wonder if we should invite Brian over for a cup of tea, so he could see that we hadn't completely erased his creation and that his own memories were still anchored somewhere physical. Chatting to a neighbour over the fence, we found out that Brian had passed away not long after he moved out. It was around this time that our grand avocado tree had started to die, and both Beau and I couldn't help but draw an eerie connection between the two events.

My home office doubles
as a prop library; white flat-
packed furniture pieces are
used in this space, but the
busyness of my things and
a growing mood wall give
the new pieces texture.

250

We love the idea
of living with one
foot in the past,
complemented by
the meaningful
things we have
collected over
the years.

Charles Barkley sits pretty
in front of a photographic
print by Kara Rosenlund
titled *Chicken*; a colourful
abstract by David Peddle
hangs on the adjacent wall.

The power of lighting
in the home

Have you noticed how light can influence your mood and focus? In a stage performance, key moments are emphasised with a shift in light intensity or colour. Our attention is directed; the lighting design becomes a part of the narrative, reinforcing the feelings that are being expressed on the stage or forewarning the plot twists ahead. Lighting affects our emotional reading of a situation and space, but so often it is something that we don't pay much attention to in our home.

There are three layers of light to consider in our homes: *ambient lighting* provides overall illumination of a room, *task lighting* is practical lighting positioned for a specific job (for example, food preparation, reading, study) and *accent lighting* highlights details such as an artwork or a vignette on a sideboard. The key to an inviting, warm space is to find a balance between all three types of lighting.

A house evenly lit by rows and rows of downlights will not feel as intimate as a home that features different light sources, positioned at varied heights. When a space is layered with lighting, our eyes dance between the light and shadow, and we are drawn deeper into the room. The atmosphere becomes rich with highlights and lowlights, and a magical sense of depth is created.

In my grandmother's home, a textured lamp always sat on the hallway table near the front door. The base of the lamp was a knot of rich timber, and the shade was made of oatmeal wool that had been loosely woven. As soon as the sun started to drop, Grandma would switch on the lamp; the glowing entryway inevitably set the tone for the warm and cosy house beyond. This memory has shaped how I light my own home, in that I want every room to feel like it is giving you a big, enveloping hug. Lamps are dotted throughout the rooms, while wall sconces throw light onto our warm cedar-panelled wall; this creates a comfortable space from which it is difficult to tear myself away.

Layered lighting draws us into the space and makes our eyes dance between light and shadow.

Five bright ideas

1 Adding lamps to your room is an easy way to manipulate the lighting situation without needing an electrician. Floor lamps and table lamps will set a mood, act like decoration and are easy to reposition.

2 Update your wall and ceiling fittings to completely change the look of your space. Make a statement with a sculptural pendant light or an ornamental wall sconce; they will add drama to your space, even when the light is switched off.

3 Unique vintage light fittings and lamps will add character, but make sure an electrician checks the wiring before you use them.

4 A lamp doesn't have to sit on a tabletop or sideboard—I love seeing lamps on kitchen benches or snuggled into a bookcase.

5 When it comes to globes, consider both the colour temperature and the energy-efficiency rating. Warm, yellowish light is perfect for spaces in which you want to relax, whereas cool, white light suits areas that require bright, clean illumination, such as kitchens and bathrooms.

Thank you...

To all the amazing humans that opened up their homes and shared their lives with us: Adam Powell and Nick Bond; Annie Werner, Genevieve Derwent, Olive and Oscar Rose; David Whitworth; Eryca Green and Eddy Opmanis; the Fletcher family—Dannielle, Arron, Molly and Lola; Gabrielle McGrath and Michael Jarochowicz; Georgina Stuart and Matthew Quigley, with Donny and Ada Quigley; the Gilbert family—Cassy, Michael ('Gil'), Ivy and Gypsy; Helene Athanasiadis and Quilla Diaz; Leah Hudson-Smith and Wally Maloney; Matthew Lucas; Sandra Eterovic; Sarah Andrews; and Sarah and Phil Webb. The warm and cheerful spirit of the book is a reflection of the authentic, down-to-earth nature of each of you; it is a celebration of the things that make you all so great. I hope, from the bottom of my heart, that you love the way we told your story.

To David Patston and the Eterovic family, for allowing us to include your beautiful Sandra in the book. Sue and I are honoured that we have been given the opportunity to contribute to the collected memories of such a special and talented individual.

To Beau Sherrard, for keeping our home life on track while I travelled for shoots or locked myself in a room to write. Your patience, kindness and strength are among the many reasons I love you. Thanks to Charles Barkley, too—your cheeky face and funny ways never fail to calm me down in stressful moments.

To my family and friends. I apologise for the celebrations I missed, the catch-up phone calls I didn't make, or the times I sat dazed and distant at your dining table, consumed by the book and on another planet. To Mum and Dad—and my in-laws, Gail and Graham—thank you for everything, always.

To my Temple & Webster family, for the opportunities I have been given during my time as Head of Styling, learning from and working with some of the most talented people in the business. To the Creative Team in particular, whom I can always count on for limitless laughs and endless idea bouncing. Chris Deal—we will make a book together one day, and it will be bloody genius.

To Kay Scarlett, for playing such an important part in the book's early development. Thank you for your belief in the book, even when it was just a handful of images and a loose idea.

To Karen McCartney, for being a continual source of inspiration—starting back at your *Inside Out* magazine days—and for introducing me to Jane Morrow.

To my brilliant team at Murdoch Books, which has been so supportive and a delight with which to collaborate. To my publisher, Jane Morrow, I have felt incredibly safe in your hands. The same applies to Editorial Manager Julie Mazur Tribe and Design Manager Megan Pigott; thank you for your skilful direction and for shaping the content with such care. And thank you to my patient editor, Dannielle Viera, and thoughtful designer, Madeleine Kane; you have worked the words and images into exactly the kind of book I had in my head and made it a trillion times better.

And finally, to photographer Sue Stubbs. There is no doubt that your heart is bound into this book. I am eternally grateful for your gritty commitment, and I love that nothing gets in your way. You are my conspirer, travel buddy and trusted sounding board. This book began as a spark of an idea between us, and we ran with it all the way to the end. We did it. Now, let's get cracking on book number two!

Published in 2019 by Murdoch Books, an imprint of Allen & Unwin

Murdoch Books Australia
83 Alexander Street, Crows Nest NSW 2065
Phone: +61 (0)2 8425 0100
murdochbooks.com.au
info@murdochbooks.com.au

Murdoch Books UK
Ormond House, 26–27 Boswell Street, London WC1N 3JZ
Phone: +44 (0) 20 8785 5995
murdochbooks.co.uk
info@murdochbooks.co.uk

For corporate orders and custom publishing contact our business development team
at salesenquiries@murdochbooks.com.au

Publisher: Jane Morrow
Design Manager: Megan Pigott
Editorial Manager: Julie Mazur Tribe
Designer: Madeleine Kane
Editor: Dannielle Viera
Photographer: Sue Stubbs
Stylist: Jessica Bellef
Production Director: Lou Playfair

ISBN 978 1 76052 488 3 Australia
ISBN 978 1 91163 239 9 UK

A cataloguing-in-publication entry is available from the catalogue of the National Library
of Australia at nla.gov.au
A catalogue record for this book is available from the British Library

Colour reproduction by Splitting Image Colour Studio Pty Ltd, Clayton, Victoria
Printed by C&C Offset Printing Co Ltd, China